THEN SINGS MY SOUL

REDISCOVERING GOD'S PURPOSES FOR SINGING IN CHURCH

PHILIP PERCIVAL

Then Sings My Soul

Matthias Media
(St Matthias Press Ltd ACN 067 558 365)
Email: info@matthiasmedia.com.au
Internet: www.matthiasmedia.com.au
Please visit our website for current postal and telephone contact information.

Matthias Media (USA)
Email: sales@matthiasmedia.com
Internet: www.matthiasmedia.com
Please visit our website for current postal and telephone contact information.

ISBN 978 1 922206 73 2

Cover design and typesetting by Lankshear Design.

To my dearest wife, Kate

To my dearest wife, Cate

CONTENTS

Introduction	7
1. True worship	13
2. The word in song	41
3. If life were a musical…	61
4. I feel good: music and emotion	83
5. Leading song	109
6. The final song	123
7. Appendix 1: Deliberate song leading	129
8. Appendix 2: Issues for churches	137
9. Appendix 3: Idolatry in church music	147
10. Appendix 4: Church musicians	151
Acknowledgements	155

INTRODUCTION

The game was a sell-out, though you would never have guessed it.

…

There were no queues, no turnstiles and certainly no hotdog stands or programme sellers.

But once inside it was a different matter. Every seat was taken and row upon row of men sat silently, wearing identical dark suits and red ties, everyone sporting a tiny enamel badge on their left breast.

No, not of Pyongyang FC, but of the Great Leader himself.

The artificial pitch looked immaculate under the spring morning sun. Kick off was at half past nine.

Maybe it was the early start but there were no chants and no flags or scarves in sight, just a quiet murmur around the darkened rows of seats.

Many of the fans were soldiers in green uniforms and broad-brimmed hats.

I do not know if they were under orders to attend but some were quietly reading paperbacks and showed no interest in the game.

The opposition, the crack army outfit Amrokgang, looked stronger in the first half but it was a scrappy match.

Pyongyang fought back and won a penalty though you would be hard pressed to know that from the reaction of the crowd. There was none.

...

Back on the pitch at the Kim Il-Sung stadium, Amrokgang had got one back.

[But] the goal caused little reaction. The crowd stayed quiet. Neither manager ventured out of the dugout, there was no high-fiving, no pats on the back from the players.

Now I like to watch controlled football, but not quite like this...[1]

This is a part of a genuine report from the BBC of a 2013 football match in North Korea, where games are staged for no other reason than putting on a show. Sadly, it reminds me of some church services I have been to. Okay, maybe this is a bit of a

1 T Hartley, 'North Korea's silent football matches', *BBC News*, 11 May 2013 (viewed 5 June 2015): www.bbc.com/news/magazine-22470430.

stark exaggeration. But I am sure we have all had times where we look around at people gathered at church and wonder if anyone is actually feeling anything at all.

Now just in case you are worried that you have picked up the wrong book, don't worry. This book *is* about singing in church! And I assume you are reading it because you have some sort of interest in the subject—you're a musician, or a pastor, or someone who takes church gatherings seriously. Great! But if excellent church music were just a matter of playing to a high standard, then all you would need to do is get your musicians some lessons and ask them to practise a lot. The problem would still be, however, that it would look just like that North Korean football match. The excellence of the music would not necessarily create a response. And this is the case whether your church has a beautiful choir, a great band, hands in the air, or hands in pockets.

Of course, if you've ever been part of some really great Christian singing, you'll know that there is much more to it than simply the quality of the band, the organ or the singers at the front. One aim of this book is to figure out what those x-factor qualities are that make singing in church one of life's greatest experiences. But this is only a part of what we're doing, and I would suggest that in some ways it's not even that important!

Yes, we all love great singing in church. But can you imagine doing singing in a way that transforms your understanding of God's amazing redeeming purposes for the world? Can you imagine doing singing in a way that can totally reshape the way you live? Can you imagine doing singing in a way that engages both heart and mind—stirring the affections of the soul in a way that is authentic, true and godly?

Well, these are big questions for a small book, but they are actually the very things the Bible encourages in our singing. Because when Christians sing, we are plugging into God's designs for his church. Singing helps us know and feel the truth; it can train us in godly living. It is about us being intimate with the creator of all things.

And this takes us back to the question of why, when so many Christians gather together each week and the singing starts, there can often be so little sign of life. It might be to do with how the music is led and played. But I would argue that more often than not it is actually because we have forgotten what it is to be alive—because in a perverted way it feels safer for us not to feel anything rather than to truly engage with the Lord of the universe and with each other. When your affections are moved by the gospel you begin to become alive to Christ Jesus and are prepared to live radically and passionately for him. And that, for many Christians, may just seem too frightening.

That's what this book is about: getting singing right because we genuinely love Jesus; getting singing right in order that the gospel might infect our hearts and minds, so that we might be faithful and passionate servants of God.

To do this, our thinking may need to be challenged

in many areas—like how we understand church and worship. It will involve looking at the Bible so we understand how the gospel affects our feelings, and how we should be leading others in singing the gospel. It will be a scary thing for some to rethink music in this way. But changing how we sing to reflect God's purposes will, he promises, transform lives for his glory.

1. TRUE WORSHIP

A woman walks by herself, in the heat of the day, along a dusty road. The reason she is on her own is that she has failed at life. Things weren't meant to have turned out like this. She just wants what everyone else has: love, intimacy and affection. But her longings and desires for these things have only ever got her into trouble. In fact every attempt to find love has failed. Every relationship ends in disaster. And her behaviour has grown more and more compulsive and destructive—so much so that she is now an outcast from society. She has five broken marriages behind her and now lives with someone who uses her as much as she uses him. Yet still she craves real love more than ever.

She knows about God. In fact when she gave up on finding love from others, she tried religion. She knows that God is somehow meant to understand her emptiness and bring satisfaction to her longings. She knows the stories about God's promised redeemer. But here again she has failed. Attempts to be religious felt good at the time, but she always walked away from worship as empty as ever. God just felt too distant, his promises faint. And in the cheap affection of her many lovers she could at least pretend that she knew intimacy, though the pain of emptiness never left her heart.

She has known a lot of men. But none like the one she would meet this day. She is out in the heat of the day because only then can she use the village well without being noticed. Yet today she is not alone. Sitting at the well is a stranger. He is clearly not one of her own people… maybe a traveller? This man looks as though he is waiting for something, or someone. But as she approaches, she notices his eyes are fixed on her. "Will you give me a drink?" he asks. A strange request. But as he continues speaking it seems, oddly, more like he's offering *her* something to drink—which is totally inconceivable, particularly if he knows the truth about who she is. But this is no ordinary man and he is offering no ordinary drink. As she finds herself listening to the strangest things about drinking and being satisfied, her heart starts to warm for the first time. And as someone who has spent her life craving to be filled with something more than just guilt, she finds herself pleading with this man she has just met, to give her some of this life-changing drink he is offering.

But then things came unstuck. He starts asking questions. "Where is your husband?" Unless she lies, he too will cast her off as worthless. "I have no husband", she confesses. And to her surprise, he tells her that he knows all about her past relationships. Thinking that this man must be a prophet of some sort, she tries to impress him with her knowledge of religion and worship. But again, he twists what she is trying to say. And now *he* is describing worship in a way that is unlike any experience of religion she has ever had. "God is Spirit", he says. "And his worshippers must worship in spirit and in truth…"

As we come to think through the issues of worship, music and the church, I want us to be in the same place as this broken and desperate woman. What I have been retelling is the story, in John 4, of Jesus' meeting with a Samaritan woman—a most unlikely conversation between two unlikely people. Yet this is essentially *my* story. And it is the story of all whose souls are thirsty to be filled with the real, intimate and deeply satisfying love of our creator. This story reflects my failure to know what it is to love and be loved. It speaks of my longing to find satisfaction in the deepest parts of my heart. It describes Jesus' offer of life to those who are broken, and his demands on those who take up this offer. And he does this by pointing to true worship.

But hang on a minute. That all sounds great, but what has this got to do with the 'worship' in my church and in my life? And what does it have to do with singing? If worship is about God satisfying my unfulfilled desires and failed longings, then how does that help me with how I do music in church? Well, we'll think about that in a moment. However, let me say upfront: in the

Bible, worship never simply equals singing. And for that matter, singing is never described as worship. What we *do* see, however, is that true worship is much bigger than all the things that can happen in a church service.

And yet singing *does* have a profound role in the lives of those who are true worshippers of God. On its own, singing can never satisfy those desires that only true worship can. However, singing *is* the language of our affections. And it is used by God to plant the word of Christ in the hearts of those who long to be touched, filled and changed by his perfect love.

So what am I saying? That singing is not worship, and worship is not the things we do in church, and yet somehow both these things are part of God's plan to satisfy our deepest longings and desires? Yes—it's complicated! So let's press on and work it out, leaving at the door all our preconceptions in order to let God's word inform and inspire a fresh understanding of worship, the church, our hearts, and singing.

Words for worship

First of all we have to make some sort of sense of what true worship actually is. How do you understand worship? Is it something you do? Is it about how you feel when you do 'religion'? Is it about approaching God in the right way? Is it something you do to please him? Or is it actually just a way to describe the Sunday service? Is it the singing part of the service? Or is it the slow reflective bit of the singing part of the service? Most of us have been so conditioned by thinking about 'worship' in these sorts of ways that it can become all too easy to read our own meanings back into the Bible, and yet still have no real clue about how to worship God the way he intends.

None of this is helped by the problem of language. 'Worship' is an English word which means 'to offer someone honour and respect', the way you might treat someone greater than yourself—like the Queen, or your favourite football player, or even someone you are in love with. The Bible, however, wasn't originally written in English. In our translations, 'worship' is actually used to translate a whole range of different words found in the Hebrew and Greek. In reading our modern Bibles, as good as they are, you won't always know what is behind the word 'worship' when you see it written down.

Why is this so important? It's important because many of us try to worship God by being 'religious'. When we get worship wrong—when we turn worship into 'religion'—we very quickly start to undermine the gospel of grace. As soon as we start to approach God on our own terms to please him or gain blessing by doing religious acts, we start to deny the power of the cross to make us right with God. And there are plenty of churches out there where worship to some degree equals music—delivered in a way to help us experience God without the need for the death and resurrection of Jesus. So to avoid this danger we need to go back to the beginning with worship—to understand the Bible's worship language in order to look towards the amazing reality to which it all points.

Worship as honour

a. Bowing with attitude

The way we normally think of worship is in terms of offering someone (or something) honour and respect. The Bible pretty much thinks in this way too. The Greek word for this is the verb *proskynein*. Originally *proskynein* described the physical act of bowing down before someone:[2]

> Then Moses and Aaron went and gathered together all the elders of the people of Israel. Aaron spoke all the words that the LORD had spoken to Moses and did the signs in the sight of the people. And the people believed; and when they heard that the LORD had visited the people of Israel and that he had seen their affliction, they bowed their heads and worshipped. (Exod 4:29-31)

Moses and the elders instinctively responded to the revelation of God in his word and actions by physically worshipping. Most translations will use both 'bowing' and

2 The Bible also has a number of other related worship words to do with fear and reverence, which we won't look at here but which are still broadly related to the idea of offering God honour and respect.

'worshipping'—which is a bit strange as the writer seems to be using two words that essentially mean the same thing. But this is all about saying that there is both action and intent in the worship. That is, as they bowed down they showed the honour they felt towards God. As the Bible later shows us, an action towards God (e.g. offering a sacrifice—Ps 51:16-17) means nothing on its own. It's all about what is going on in your heart when you do it.

b. Attitude without bowing

Because what happens in the heart is as important as the action itself, it is quite common for the Bible writers to use worship in the *abstract* sense alone (that is, without the actual bowing down). This is what you and I normally do when we talk about worshipping someone. For example:

> Worship the LORD in the splendour of holiness;
> tremble before him, all the earth! (Ps 96:9)

In this psalm, the whole earth is called to worship God in response to who he is and what he has done. And while worship here still captures the idea of bowing, it is quite clear that the earth itself can't literally do that. The intent of this psalm, then, is to describe the *attitude* God requires from all who dwell on the earth: honour, respect and reverent fear—all of which leads to the offering of praise and the rejection of idolatry.

c. Bowing in response to Jesus

In the New Testament, something really interesting happens to *proskynein* worship. Whereas any old idol, king or whatever could be bowed to in the Old Testament, in the Gospels, *proskynein* worship is almost always directed towards Jesus. It's not that the first-century football players wouldn't have had fans worshipping them. But to the writers of the New Testament, Jesus Christ was the only true object of man's worship. There is no other that deserves this act of honour—which makes complete sense when we remember that the Gospel writers' main task is to convince us that Jesus of Nazareth is actually God himself:

> Now after Jesus was born in Bethlehem of Judea in the days of Herod the king, behold, wise men from the east came to Jerusalem, saying, "Where is he who has been born king of the Jews? For we saw his star when it rose and have come to worship him." (Matt 2:1-2)

> Jesus immediately reached out his hand and took hold of him [Peter], saying to him, "O you of little faith, why did you doubt?" And when they got into the boat, the wind ceased. And those in the boat worshipped him, saying, "Truly you are the Son of God". (Matt 14:31-33)

These examples show that physical worship is driven by an attitude of reverence—once shown by Moses and Israel towards God, but now directed at Jesus. What has changed is that God has become flesh; and it is not just the nation of Israel that worships him but also representatives of the Gentile nations.

Going further into the New Testament, the picture becomes even clearer. In Revelation 5 the elders fall down before the one seated on the throne and before the Lamb. Likewise, in Philippians 2:9-11, Paul presents the image of every knee being moved to bow before Jesus—in many ways the fulfilment of Psalm 96's call to worship. God the Father honours Jesus in bringing all creation to submission before him. And as marvellous as this is, what is frightening is the implication that *all* the earth will be forced to bow before Jesus—whether willingly or not, whether in joy or terror.

d. Bowing in spirit

In the New Testament, then, Jesus becomes the ultimate object of worship. But there is one significant passage that shows that he is not just the *object* of our worship, but is also the *means* of our worshipping. This brings us back to John chapter 4, where we left unanswered the question of how worship can satisfy our deepest needs. Well, it's here that the Bible pushes worship to its furthest point, and we most clearly see what worship means for you and me. Jesus himself states that true worship is not a physical but a spiritual activity. To the Samaritan woman he says that God does not want us to worship him at (or in) a particular place, but "in spirit and in truth". It is something we do not in a church, a temple, on a mountain or in a desert—but spiritually.[3] Which is great! Except at first it feels like Jesus never properly explains what worshipping "in spirit and truth" actually looks like. Of course if we look closer, it starts to become clear that Jesus is talking about himself. In John's Gospel the question of 'what is truth' is always answered by looking at Jesus himself (e.g. Jesus comes from God, full of grace and *truth*—1:14; Jesus is the way, the *truth* and the life—14:6).

To worship God *in this life* does not now mean physically bowing before him (even though that's what all creation is one day going to do). Christian worship happens in an even more profound way: in our hearts. This worship transcends any earthly ritual, action or performance—no matter how religious they may seem—because it flows out of hearts that are transformed by Christ. Only those who accept his offer of living water—who find their satisfaction in him and who are born again of the Spirit—will have a renewed heart of flesh that genuinely honours the Lord of creation. Our lives don't revolve around a weekly sacrifice in a temple—but we continually and perpetually honour God by virtue of being in Christ, our worship bound to him by *his* once-for-all and perfect sacrifice on the cross.

So true worship is spiritual, and is fundamentally tied

3 It is worth pointing out that there are two possible meanings for worshipping "in spirit". One is 'in the Holy Spirit', which would make sense in light of the other language in John about being born again in the Spirit. The other is 'in *our* spirit', or 'spiritually'.

to our salvation in Christ. On account of the cross, those in Christ spiritually bow before the Creator. Of course, those who seek to satisfy their desires in this world will only ever worship the things of this world—whether it be the longed-for perfect relationship, or the self-worth of a successful career, or the shallow pursuit of cheap pleasure. However, those who drink from the well that never runs dry are the worshippers God seeks. They find their satisfaction in him. And their worship belongs to him.[4]

If worship is so profoundly tied to us being *in Christ*—in a way that drives the core attitude of our hearts to God—then this has to make us question why we are so easily prepared to describe our church services as acts of worship, our buildings as places of worship, our songs as worship offerings, and our singers as worship leaders. We'll think more about this in a moment.

Summary

The New Testament helps us to understand worship in two key ways. On the one hand we see that God is moving history to the point where the whole of creation will submit to Jesus, the Lord of all creation. All people will bow before him, both friends and enemies. Alongside that is the idea that true worship is essentially spiritual—that genuine engagement with God requires Jesus giving

4 If you are interested, go and have a look at Jeremiah 2:13, which describes Israel's sin of idolatry using the image of drinking water from cracked cisterns. Jesus' gift of living water, in contrast, is offered to those whose worship of God is through him alone.

us new hearts. Just as Jesus restores our relationship with God, broken at the fall, so he restores our actions and affections towards God. Worship is therefore fundamentally about the attitude of our hearts. And without the transformation that Jesus offers, we can never approach God with the genuine honour he demands from his creation. In saving me Jesus replaces my corrupted heart, with all of its longings for worldly satisfaction, with one that finds delight in honouring the Lord of creation.

FURTHER THOUGHTS...

A wonderful part of our lives of grace is that we can offer the 'fruit of our lips' (Heb 13:15) in praise to God. God *delights* in this. Our praise, however, is not what is at the heart of true worship. (We'll come back to what praise is later.) Worship fundamentally concerns our standing with God. We approach God *in Christ*, the attitude of our hearts restored when we are filled with his Spirit.

So you can't worship God by singing, "I worship you!", even if that is what you are feeling in your heart at the time. In fact, you won't find such a phrase in the Bible; nor similar expressions such as, "We come before you in worship". When the Bible speaks of worship, it is either as a description of someone approaching God or Christ (e.g. "We have come to worship him"), or it is a 'call to worship' (e.g. "Worship the LORD in the splendour of holiness"). It is not something you do by saying you're doing it! Worship is a much more profound and fundamental part of our relationship with the Creator. For those in Christ, worship happens whether or not you are feeling good, or righteous, or sad, or distant. Praise God that true worship is not all about us!

Worship as service (in all of life)

If someone claims to be in love with you, you would expect to see some expression of that love in the things they do, like buying you flowers or taking you out for a romantic meal. Those actions on their own are nice things, but what makes them special is the love that inspires and drives them. That's a bit like how worship in Christ drives the rest of our life.

We said earlier that the Bible has a number of different words that can be translated as 'worship'. Perhaps the most important one to know about, apart from *proskynein*, is *latruein*—the Greek word that often means 'to serve', and which is essentially *the expression* of our hearts of worship.

a. A life of worship

Serving God does sound a bit like worshipping God, and there are many occasions where worshipping and serving sit right next to each other in the Scriptures. For example:

> And Jesus answered him [Satan], "It is written,
>
> "'You shall worship the Lord your God,
> and him only shall you serve.'" (Luke 4:8)

But there is a subtle, though distinct, difference between worship and service (like there is a difference between being in love and buying someone flowers). If worship is the attitude of my heart, then service is the practical outworking of my worship. That is, I show my honour for God by being obedient to him in all my actions; by *serving* him. You see this in the classic Old Testament command:

> "Hear, O Israel: The Lord our God, the Lord is one. You shall love the Lord your God with all your heart and with all your soul [worship] and with all your might [service]." (Deut 6:4-5)

This was how the people of Israel, the nation saved by grace, were to live out their lives. With worshipping hearts they were to serve God in everything, both within their religious activities and in their day-to-day lives:

> "And when the Lord your God brings you into the land that he swore to your fathers, to Abraham, to Isaac, and to Jacob, to give you… then take care lest you forget the Lord, who brought you out of the land of Egypt, out of the

> house of slavery. It is the LORD your God you shall fear. Him you shall serve and by his name you shall swear." (Deut 6:10, 12-13)

> "You shall not make for yourself a carved image, or any likeness of anything that is in heaven above, or that is in the earth beneath, or that is in the water under the earth. You shall not bow down to them or serve them..." (Exod 20:4-5)

In the New Testament, nothing really changes. The key verse that picks this up is Romans 12:1:

> I appeal to you therefore, brothers, by the mercies of God, to present your bodies as a living sacrifice, holy and acceptable to God, which is your rational service.[5]

In the argument of Romans, 'reasonable' or 'rational' service is how *we* are to live out our response to the gospel. The logic is this: By God's grace you are saved by faith. Therefore, just as Israel offered its ritual sacrifices, you now offer your bodies as living sacrifices in service to God. This is the right response to being saved. Our service, however, is not performed in a ritual but is to be an all-encompassing part of our otherwise 'ordinary' lives.

So just as the people of Israel were to fear and serve God in everything because they were a nation saved by grace, so it is with us. And the really important thing to

5 See the ESV footnote for translation notes.

note here is that our service is a *response* to being saved, not something that *makes* us saved.

b. Where it gets messy...

Romans 12:1 is a significant instance where clarity about the meaning of 'worship' is lost because the underlying word is obscured in translation. Many of us will know this verse in terms of it speaking of our "spiritual worship". This would be great if Paul were talking about the same thing as Jesus in John 4 (where Jesus is redefining the way we approach God—i.e. through himself). But he isn't! And without going back over the differences between worship and service again, a serious implication of translating Romans 12:1 as "spiritual worship" is that it can unhelpfully promote the idea that there is a special category of 'gathered worship'—even if that is the exact opposite of Jesus' teaching on spiritual worship in John 4.

Of course there is plenty of 'religious ritual' in the Bible. But, as we shall see in a moment, the New Testament uses ritual language in a deliberate and careful way that manages to pick up all the exciting things the Old Testament has to say about Christ and the church without ever undermining our salvation by grace.

If there is one big danger with the concept of 'gathered worship', it is that over the years many Christians have ended up putting too much weight on responding to salvation in liturgical (or 'churchy') terms—a weight that was never meant to be there. In this way of thinking it is all too easy to let singing, for example, take on the role of a sacrificial gift, requiring all the dignity and reverence that such offerings require. We will get to the place of singing in the church (eventually). But let's be clear—this is not at all what Romans 12 is about. Read the rest of chapter 12 and you'll see that Paul isn't talking about church meetings at all. Rather, our 'reasonable service' is all about loving others!

Worship as ritual

There are times in life where getting dramatic helps to make a point—like when a child fakes being ill in order to get attention from its parent. Or when the Formula One champion shakes and opens an oversized bottle of champagne. Or when the preacher starts pounding the lectern with his fist to show his passion for what he is preaching. Drama within an otherwise ordinary situation helps to make a point! And there is an element of that in what God asked the people of Israel to do in their service of him.

As we have seen, Israel was to serve God in every part of the nation's life. But God also wanted them to 'act out' part of that service—in the performance of religious rituals. This was not a trivial matter. The rituals connected with the temple, sacrifices and priesthood were all part of an elaborate system for Israel to recognize and deal with the ongoing problem of sin. Now, it is crucial to remember that the sacrificial system only operated under the umbrella of God's grace. That is, Israel was already God's saved people. The Israelites could not make themselves more saved by offering sacrifices. But in doing so they were to take both God's holiness and their own sin seriously. And, as God often reminded them, it was not the actual sacrifice that would please him so much as the repentant hearts that should lie behind such offerings:

> Open my lips, Lord,
> and my mouth will declare your praise.
> You do not delight in sacrifice, or I would bring it;
> you do not take pleasure in burnt offerings.
> My sacrifice, O God, is a broken spirit;
> a broken and contrite heart
> you, God, will not despise. (Ps 51:15-17, NIV)

It would be really hard to see the relevance of this whole system if the New Testament wasn't so clear in showing us that these rituals prefigured something that Jesus would come and do perfectly. In fact, it is this very imagery that is regularly used by the New Testament writers to explain the profound nature of the gospel and salvation.

a. The temple

When God established the tabernacle (under Moses) and later the temple (under Solomon), it was to show that he lived among his people. However, while the temple demonstrated God's nearness, it also showed his distance. For once inside the temple gates, there were a number of barriers you needed to get past in order to get near to God. In fact, only the High Priest could enter the Most Holy Place to intercede for the people, and only once a year.

Yet all the design, architecture and engineering of these great structures had but one purpose—to prepare us for God's ultimate act of grace towards us. We read in John 1:14 that "the Word became flesh and dwelt [literally, 'tabernacled'] among us, and we have seen his glory". God's glory (which was hidden even from Moses) was revealed in Jesus—as God came to live among his people—without any barriers. John also explains how Jesus himself replaced the physical temple (John 2:19-21), in doing so showing that the place to meet God is not in a building but in the person of Christ!

b. The sacrifices

The centrepiece of the Old Covenant ritual system was the sacrifice of atonement—the offering of the blood of an animal to pay for the sins committed by the people of Israel. In Romans, however, Paul states that it was always God's plan that Jesus, in his death, would become the perfect atoning sacrifice [literally, 'propitiation'] for the sins of humanity:

> …for all have sinned and fall short of the glory of God, and are justified by his grace as a gift, through the redemption that is in Christ Jesus, whom God put forward as a propitiation by his blood, to be received by faith. (Rom 3:23-25)

c. The priests

The role of the priest was to be an intermediary between Israel and God. The priests were the ones who could offer the sacrifices necessary for cleansing Israel's sin. Hebrews 10 shows us again that Jesus fulfils this role perfectly:

> Therefore, brothers, since we have confidence to enter the holy places by the blood of Jesus, by the new and living way that he opened for us through the curtain, that is, through his flesh, and since we have a great priest over the house of God, let us draw near with a true heart in full assurance of faith, with our hearts sprinkled clean from an evil conscience and our bodies washed with pure water. (Heb 10:19-22)

As high priest, Jesus offers the single perfect sacrifice for sin, allowing us to enter the heavenly sanctuary (the eternal kingdom of God) with confidence and with renewed hearts.

In fact, Hebrews shows us that if you wanted to satisfy God in the religious sort of way, there is only one person who could ever actually do it: Jesus. Hebrews 8:6 uses yet another word related to worship, *leitourgos*, to describe Jesus in this priestly role (although it's also the word that we get liturgy from!).

d. How it all fits together

So how does the Bible as a whole handle this ritualized form of service worship? It uses it to point to, and explain, the life and work of Jesus. Hebrews and other parts of the New Testament go out of their way to show how the Old Testament sacrificial system was part of God's brilliant plan to help us understand the cross. But equally they explain Jesus' ongoing role in providing this ministry for us as our high priest. All those things that Israel had to do (basically anything to do with temples, priests and sacrifices) *stopped* at Jesus, when he perfectly became those objects for our sake.

e. How it all falls apart

Where things can get confusing, however, is in the way the New Testament writers continue to use ritualistic language to paint pictures of what life and service in church is all about. There are many examples, like the church being described as the temple of the Holy Spirit (1 Cor 6:19) or as a royal priesthood (1 Pet 2:9); or offering our bodies and the fruit of our lips as sacrifices (Rom 12:1; Heb 13:15). These passages use those rich images of the Old Testament ritual service to help us understand—as they were to help Israel understand—what it means to live righteous lives under the umbrella of God's grace. What they don't do is say that Christians still operate under a ritualistic system. Nowhere, for example, do we see that the temple is simply replaced by church buildings or services. (Yes, the church is described as the temple of the Holy Spirit—but we'll look at that in the next chapter!)

Sadly, it seems as if much of the early Christian church didn't quite get it, and thereby created a legacy of 'religious' worship that lingers on today.

Where have we gone wrong?

Church history shows us that soon after the New Testament was written, Christians started to forget that Jesus was the perfect fulfilment of worship, service and Old Testament ritual. Liturgy (the thing that Jesus brought to perfect completion!) became all-important in Christian meetings. Ritual replaced gathering for edification and service. Church became a performance, and the Lord's Supper became the focus of these performances as Jesus' body and blood were systematically *re-offered* to God as an atonement for our sins. Jesus' perfect work on the cross had soon become not so perfect.

By the Middle Ages, the ongoing theatre of religious ritual had become what we would describe as mystical. Mysticism in the medieval church involved *experiencing* God. Without having an assurance of faith based on God's grace alone, the mystics set about creating a spiritual atmosphere to make people feel that God was there and that they were okay with him. While this sort of thing was not at all the purpose of the Old Testament temple/priest/sacrifice system, it certainly provided a nice religious model to follow. Where better to stage a performance of priests offering sacrifices than in a great temple—the cathedral? And it wasn't just about the religious theatre that went on up the front. In this kind of church you could engage all the senses: taste, as you ate the Lord's Supper (the bread anyway—you had to be a priest to drink the wine); light—magnificent colours pouring through huge stained-glass windows; smell—the intoxicating perfume of the incense; and, of course, sound. With a choir of monks in a cathedral you'd hear the mesmerizing and ethereal sound of plainsong chanting. You wouldn't have understood it because it was in Latin, but it would have sounded impressive never the less. All these things would have blown away the average peasant in the Middle Ages—and not just the ones over 40. You would truly have thought you were entering another dimension as you entered 'God's holy place'.

Singing, therefore, was a key ingredient of the liturgy. It helped create the mystical experience that God's 'temple' was meant to evoke. And in many ways this legacy is carried on in many churches today. Even the Reformers did not think anything much about this general attitude towards viewing church gatherings as acts of worship. It is common for protestant churches today to still refer to church meetings as 'Divine Worship' or the 'Worship Service'. Others will still refer to parts of the building as the sanctuary, or will have altars and priests and more.

More worrying than churches using the language

of the temple, however, is the fact that some churches continue to put on the mystical show—complete with lighting and smoke machines. By hanging on to the notion of the church building as 'God's house', they conclude that God's house needs to be filled with 'God's presence'. So, like the medieval church, they keep adding in that something extra to be sure that God is present in the service. Like the re-offering of Jesus' body each week, so is the desire to *experience* God's presence and blessing. And for many, music has become a major device to ensure that God is 'in the house'. If the singing is great then we enthrone God on the praises of his people (Ps 22:3). In reality, the singing is being used to drive people's emotions towards a state of religious ecstasy. If we feel good then God must be here, pouring out his blessings on us. If you do the music right, then you are opening the portal into heaven itself.

So whatever has brought about the modern confusion over worship, church and singing, I suspect it is as a result of the church over the years being attracted to a model of ritualistic worship based on the old covenant worship of Israel. And singing, which was designed to have a profound role in the gathering of God's people, has wrongly been caught up in the theatre of liturgical and mystical church.

What we need to remember is that nothing we do in church of a ritualistic or mystical nature can ever please or satisfy God (let alone satisfy us!). The fact that we label it as worship just helps to confuse things further.

As we will shortly see, our singing, as a ministry of God's word, is for teaching, edification and thankful response to the gospel—a result of Christ dwelling in our hearts. What it *isn't* is the key to opening the gateway into God's presence, or a sacrifice, or a good work. We cannot know the presence of God apart from knowing Jesus, who is God's glory revealed to us.

Summary

There is a lot of confusion out there about worship!

I think the reason we all like ritual, whether it be lighting candles or singing I-will-worship-you songs, is that as fallen people we will always think we have to do something to fix our sin. All of us struggle with the worship of idols as we seek to fill the void in our hearts that sin creates. Christians have at times done a great job of turning religion itself into an idol, because it is so much more tangible than simply accepting God's perfect gift of grace. We find it so hard not to think that we need to earn God's love in some way, particularly when we know we don't deserve it.

In the end, worship boils down to our basic relationship with God. We can attempt to engage with him through the mystical experiences of ritual and singing, turning 'worship' itself into idolatry. Or we can approach him through Jesus, who transforms the attitudes of our hearts towards God. In Christ we worship in spirit and in truth. In Christ our hearts are made acceptable to God aside from anything we can contribute. In Christ our hearts are enabled for service. A heart of true worship is one that looks not for satisfaction in the world or in the things we can achieve, but is instead fed and nurtured by the living water from the well that will never run dry. The cross shows us that there is nothing more beautiful, nothing greater to be experienced, nothing deeper to be understood, no desire worth pursuing more, than Christ. Worship of anything else is idolatry. It will deliver us momentary pleasure at best. At worst it will bring self-centredness, guilt and ultimately death. We were designed to worship God through Christ. And the amazing grace of the gospel is that this gift is ours for the taking:

> 'Twas grace that taught my heart to fear,
> And grace my fears relieved;
> How precious did that grace appear
> The hour I first believed![6]

All of which leaves us with these (and most likely many other) questions: If true worship is about a transformed heart in Christ, then isn't that something you would want to sing about, and doesn't that then make it a worship song? And if the Bible doesn't see worship and singing as the same thing, then what place *does* singing have in God's picture for his people?

6 J Newton, 'Amazing Grace', 1779.

FURTHER THOUGHTS...

Considering everything we have just said, we need to allow that words *can* change their meaning over time and can be understood differently in certain contexts. Today many people will have a broader concept of worship than the Bible's intention. For example, 'worship song' may simply mean a song we sing in church. What we need to watch out for though, is when we think we are doing something that is biblical when it is not; or, more specifically, when we allow people in church to believe that something mystical is going on when we gather, when it is not. When we overuse 'worship' in our language, it is possible to let 'worship' become the thing we are pursuing—by serving 'worship' because of how it makes us feel or because we love the 'liturgy' it creates; or by adoring the worship leader rather than Christ.

2. THE WORD IN SONG

On a recent holiday to Germany, some friends and I decided we would visit Wittenburg, the home of Martin Luther. But on our journey a stop for lunch landed us in the city of Leipzig. After a short walk around the city we found ourselves in front of a huge statue of JS Bach, behind which was the church where he ministered as the Director of Music. For me, this was one of those spine-tingling moments! Of all the 'great' composers, Bach has always stood out to me as special—not just because he 'invented' Western tonal harmony, but because his work was clearly done in the service of Jesus. Bach saw himself as a Christian musician, not just a musician who was a Christian. The gospel, therefore, is woven throughout much of his work. You can see this in his cantatas, a great example being 'Jesu, Joy of Man's Desiring'. (By the way, he had to come up with one of these every week!) On the one hand, Bach is busy inventing counterpoint. On the other, in the midst of all the musical complexity, sits a simple Lutheran hymn—a 'chorale' that proclaims the word of God and sets the agenda for all the music surrounding it. I spent many years of my youth reverse-engineering Bach's chorales in music theory lessons, all the time ignorant that these musical treasures contained a much greater treasure: they were written that the word of Christ would dwell richly in us.

Now I am not expecting you to love or have even listened to the music of Bach before. But those of you who have will know that the joy is not in analysing his compositional technique (apologies to musicologists!) but in the emotion stirred by its performance. Another piece you might have heard is Bach's arrangement of 'O Sacred Head, Sore Wounded' from *St Matthew's Passion*. It is set at the cross, rich and powerful in emotion, and corporately sung as a response to the gospel account of the crucifixion. God's truth, our response, and genuine emotion are what Bach understood (and mastered) about singing in church. But these weren't his ideas. They come directly from Scripture itself, which is where I want us to go now as we look at God's plan for singing for his people.

Music in the New Testament

But first, having built up your expectations, I should say that the New Testament actually gives very little space to talking about music and singing. Compared to the Old Testament, it is also quite scarce on songs. That doesn't mean, however, that singing is not important to God and the New Testament writers. It's just that there are other crucial things that need to be communicated first. So, as you probably already know, the main purpose of the Gospels is to introduce us to Jesus, God's appointed king, and to allow us to witness the cross—the fulfilment of God's plan to deal with human sin. Then you have Acts, which describes how the gospel of salvation is in fact God's gracious gift to all who will receive it. And then you have the letters of Paul and others, explaining how to live in response to this gift.

It is in this last category that we come across the place and purpose of our singing in the church; and it's the apostle Paul in particular who takes the lead on encouraging rich and emotive singing. He doesn't go into the practical details of doing music—so nowhere do we read about Paul's ideal church band or favourite songs. What a relief! Instead, he helps us to understand our singing *theologically*.

Now please don't be scared off at the mention of theology. Theology (or doctrine) is actually about making God and his ways and purposes *easy* to understand! It helps us to make sense of any passage, even the tricky ones, by reading that passage in the context of the whole story and big themes of the Bible. That's why, for example, we have doctrines of *sin*, *salvation*, *judgement*, and so on, which pull together everything that is said on the subject and then serve it up in a digestible portion. When it comes to talking about music, you will find a lot of people want do it within the doctrine of *worship*. However, as we've already seen, the biblical doctrine of worship doesn't really take us to singing. While both worship and music involve the human heart, Paul never talks about singing in the context of *worship*; he only ever talks about singing in the context of the doctrine of *the church*. It is Paul's description of the nature of the church that helps shape a theology of singing that is centred on the word of Christ and the work of the Holy Spirit.

The church

So if singing plugs into *church*, then let's think briefly about what church actually is.

Most of us have pictures on our walls—although unless you are seriously into art (or quite rich), you're more likely to have a print rather than the original artwork. I grew up far away from the great galleries of Europe, but I do remember that we always had prints of Constable and Turner and Picasso on the walls of our home. Now, while on the one hand you can say that those aren't the real pieces of art, on the other hand they kind of still are. They may not be the original paintings, but they still have all the colour and style and emotion of the real thing. Of course, when I finally got to see the originals, I was blown away by their magnificence. But those prints on the wall at home are still wonderful—and they are wonderful because they reflect something more real than themselves. It's similar with the church. Our meetings may be amazing or they may be really hard work. Either way, something special is happening: they are completely real and authentic churches, but at the same time they are reflecting a greater reality. Let me explain…

'The Church' is a big deal in the New Testament, and nowhere more so than in the letters of Paul and in Hebrews. The word 'church' in Greek (*ekklesia*) simply means an assembly, or gathering of people. It even refers to the angry mob who are going after Paul in Ephesus (see Acts 19). A correct theology of church most likely doesn't come out of the angry-mob sort of gathering—although it does remind me of a few churches I know! Rather, God's church (or assembly) has one crucial feature. It gathers around a person: Jesus Christ. Ephesians 2:4-6 tells us that when we are saved we are raised up with Christ in heaven. Hebrews 12:22 says that we have come to the heavenly Jerusalem where we join Christ's joyful assembly. Revelation 4-5 paints the picture of the saints of every nation gathered around the Lamb before the throne. The church gathers around Christ. Notice though where these verses place Jesus: *in heaven*! If you want to see the most perfect church, then according to the Bible you need to look at the one that is gathering right now, in heaven, around Jesus. (Think: the original painting hanging in the gallery!)

Okay. So what is going on then when we rock up to our Sunday services, home groups, prayer meetings, and so on? If Jesus isn't *physically* present with us, are we meeting as God's church? Well yes, we are—because we are also told that Christ is present with his people in his words, and by his Spirit (John 14:16). In fact, one of the Spirit's key roles is to point us to Jesus, enabling us to receive him and understand his words to us (John 3:34; Acts 4:31; 1 Cor 2:13; Eph 1:13, 6:17). Often you will see a New Testament letter directed to an actual group of Christians meeting in a certain place. The letter may be written either as an encouragement or because they have big problems, but there is always the assumption that the assembly is fundamentally Christ's church, led by him, and a manifestation of his perfect heavenly church. Just like the print on your wall at home—completely the real thing, but at the same time a reflection of the really real thing. That's why so many different metaphors are used to describe and encourage the church (Christ's body, the temple of the Holy Spirit, etc.)—they explain how our feeble gatherings are in fact something much more important than they may appear to be. We are, by God's amazing grace, gathered by Christ, and as such we belong to him; we are his body, his workmanship created for good works in him (Eph 2:10).

Of course, as members of Christ's body we are expected to behave accordingly. 1 Corinthians is a letter written to a church that doesn't seem to understand what it means to live the way God intended. Hence there are those classic chapters that teach us about serving each other (chapter 12); about what love really is (chapter 13); and about what's important and what's not when we meet together (chapter 14).

We could say much more about the doctrine of the church, all of which would be beneficial in figuring out biblical music ministry. But for now, let's just stick with the main ideas.

The church is people—not a building or an organization. It is an assembly of God's people gathered around and led by his son, Jesus. It is most perfect in heaven, but equally as real in our earthly gatherings when Jesus is present in his word and Spirit. Living as a member of the church has little to do with us taking part in its rituals or ceremonies, and everything to do with serving Christ and his people. We use whatever gifts we have (or don't have!) within the situations and circumstances we find ourselves. We strive to encourage and to build one another up in Christ. And we exist to offer God prayer and praise in all things. This diagram helps us see how it all works:[7]

7 Adapted from V Roberts, *True Worship*, Authentic, Milton Keynes, 2002, p. 63, citing HI Marshall, 'How far did the early Christians worship God?', *Churchman*, vol. 99, no. 3, 1985, p. 227.

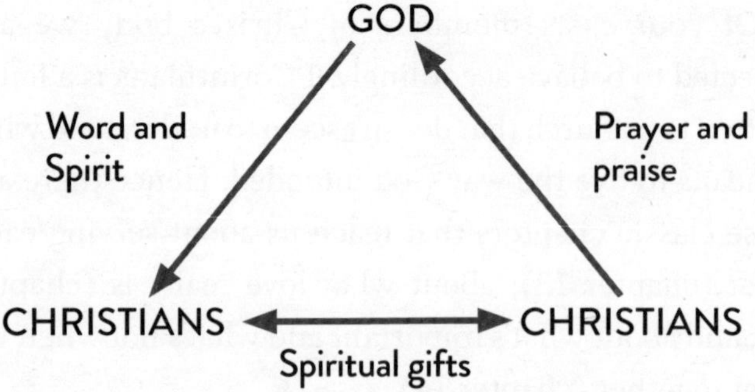

It is with this picture of the church in his mind that Paul explains singing!

Singing within the church

a. 1 Corinthians 14:26

> What then, brothers? When you come together, each one has a hymn, a lesson, a revelation, a tongue, or an interpretation. Let all things be done for building up.

This verse sets singing in the setting of the Christian meeting. It seems that it was normal for members of the Corinthian church to contribute in various ways to the time spent together, which included bringing a hymn along. Without knowing what this may have actually looked like (maybe it was sung to the gathering or maybe it was for group singing—who knows!), we can see that Paul is saying *if* you do it—because this isn't a list of compulsory things—then you do it to build up the assembly.

We need to ask, then: how is bringing along a hymn going to build up the church? I think the answer lies in looking at the other activities in this list: lessons, revelations, tongues and interpretations. Again, while I don't think we are looking at a list of compulsory items for church meetings, these things do all have one thing in common, which *is* compulsory: they are all spoken, or more specifically, 'word' ministries of some sort. When we say 'word' ministry we are talking about an activity that involves communicating God's gospel to his people and the world. (It also includes that profound idea that Christ is the ultimate expression of God's word—but there isn't the space to go into that here!) These ministries will include the obvious examples of teaching, preaching, evangelism, and so on, but will equally incorporate the less obvious ones: prophesying, speaking in and interpreting tongues, revelations, *and* singing.

"Singing—a word ministry?", you say. "But everyone talks about singing as praise and worship, don't they?" Yes, singing does allow us to express praise. But in this context singing is listed with other spoken activities that have the express purpose of building up the body. And as we go on to look at the next passage, we'll see that this 'word' focus is actually fundamental to Christian singing—and needs to be in place before we use singing to praise, pray, preach, or do anything else for that matter.

b. Colossians 3:15-17

> And let the peace of Christ rule in your hearts, to which indeed you were called in one body. And be thankful. **Let the word of Christ dwell in you richly, teaching and admonishing one another in all wisdom, singing psalms and hymns and spiritual songs, with thankfulness in your hearts to God.** And whatever you do, in word or deed, do everything in the name of the Lord Jesus, giving thanks to God the Father through him.

The first thing to notice about Colossians 3:16 is its context. Verse 15 tells us we are talking about 'church'—the body in which we are called. It sets up the idea that Christ lives in us—not just as individuals but as his community; and that because Christ lives in us we are to be thankful.

What verse 16 then does is take these ideas—the indwelling of Christ and the church's thankfulness—and gives them practical expression. And in this we gain an amazing view of God's eternal purposes: the longing for his Son to live within the hearts of his people in a way that would transform their desires, words, actions and emotions. And—get this—singing can have a key role to play in this!

So how does this work? Well, verse 16 is a bit like a tower built of blocks—each new level depends on what is built beneath it. Here, we have a series of applications built on the foundation of Christ, creating a structure that shows both the beauty of the church and the special place that singing has in God's purposes for us.

Let the word of Christ dwell in you richly

What drives this verse is the indwelling word of Christ. Just as we are to be ruled by the peace of Christ, the instrument of that rule is his word. Perhaps the best way to understand what is meant by "the word of Christ" is to think of the word *about* Christ, or the gospel itself (the good news of salvation in Christ) *and* more broadly the whole of Scripture, which points towards him. The Christian assembly is filled with Jesus, clothed in his word with a profound richness that touches every part of its life, relationships and ministry.

Teaching and admonishing one another in all wisdom

Crucially, we each have a role to play in God's ministry of Christ to us: *we all teach the word of Christ to one another.* It may be that some in the church have specific teaching roles, but there is nonetheless an inherent teaching responsibility that belongs to the whole body.

In fact Paul uses similar words in Colossians 1:28 to outline the very purpose of his own apostolic ministry: "Him we proclaim, warning everyone and teaching everyone with all wisdom, that we may present everyone mature in Christ". By implication, we too should be looking to see each other grow in maturity in Christ as we engage in the ministry of the word to one another.

Singing psalms and hymns and spiritual songs

What we then see is an immediate application of this truth: *we can all teach the word of Christ by singing it to the assembly.* Yes, we still need gifted pastors and teachers in the church, as the word is taught in a whole range of contexts. But here Paul chooses singing as a prime example of how the whole church will wisely teach, correct and encourage each other with the gospel.

With thankfulness in your hearts to God

Again we are reminded that *thankfulness* is the core affection stirred by the indwelling Christ. If Christ owns our hearts, then the first *response* to his rule will be from the heart.[8] In the next chapter we're going to look at why the saints throughout Scripture sang so much. But in short, it was because singing was often the most appropriate way to outwardly express a response to God's salvation with genuine heart-level thankfulness. Mary, for example, sings, "My *soul magnifies* the Lord… my *spirit rejoices* in God my Saviour" (Luke 1:46-47). Of course you *can* sing without the heart engaged, but within God's good design singing comes pretty close to

8 It is worth pointing out here that when the New Testament talks about the 'heart' it is speaking not purely of our emotional centre, but also of the mind and the whole inner self. We often like to separate the head from the heart in our contemporary discussions on feelings, as indeed I do at times in this book. But to sing from the heart in biblical terms is more along the lines of Psalm 103: "Bless the Lord, O my soul, and all that is within me, bless his holy name!" (v. 1).

being the most natural way to outwardly express the affections of the heart that are inspired by the gospel.

So these three characteristics—Christ dwelling in us, teaching one another in song, and responding to God with hearts of gratitude—profoundly shape Christian singing. But there is still one really big idea about singing to come—and it actually flows out of these. Teaching one another and responding with thankfulness is *how* God uses our singing to minister Jesus to us. But *why* singing is so important comes in verse 17.

And whatever you do, in word or deed, do everything in the name of the Lord Jesus, giving thanks to God the Father through him

Paul now shows us what our singing (and equally all word ministry—whether preached in a sermon or read to ourselves) is ultimately about. The word-of-Christ-in-song package is not an end in itself, but God's plan to *transform* our way of living. Remember how each application builds on the one before? Responding with thankfulness in song (in verse 16) therefore anticipates us expressing that same thankfulness in every part of our lives (in verse 17).

The implication is that authentic word-of-Christ singing trains us to be authentically thankful people—in everything. It helps us to express emotion about Jesus when we are together in church. It helps us to experience the joy of salvation when we sing the gospel truth. But while expressing thankfulness and joy in song is a totally worthy thing in itself, our singing has a greater purpose. The same emotion in our singing should be evident in our lives—in the things we say, do and think. The indwelling word of Christ does not just affect our Christian gatherings, but will also lead to transformed hearts, minds and actions. Romans 12:1 tells us that in response to the gospel we are to offer our bodies as living sacrifices in all-of-life service of God. Colossians 3:17, however, goes further—we are to be *thankful*, heart-engaged servants of God in everything. We serve our Lord not in blind obedience but with all of our being: with mind, heart and actions engaged in thankful service. Just as we submit our bodies to God, so we submit our emotions, and serve him joyfully in every situation—in plenty or in famine, in freedom or in prison. And singing with our hearts plugged in trains us to do this.

In other words, word-of-Christ singing is to lead us to godliness. If singing in the gathering is about teaching the Word and responding in thanks, it is equally about equipping us to engage the heart in every part of life as we live for Jesus.

c. Ephesians 5:18-21

> And do not get drunk with wine… but be filled
> with the Spirit, addressing one another in
> psalms and hymns and spiritual songs, singing
> and making melody to the Lord with your

heart, giving thanks always and for everything to God the Father in the name of our Lord Jesus Christ, submitting to one another out of reverence for Christ.

In Colossians, Paul views church singing as foremost a ministry of the word of Christ in order to effect God's transforming work in our lives. You might then expect to see those same ideas repeated in the other key New Testament 'singing' passage: Ephesians 5. And at first glance you will see big similarities: that we sing to one another, that we sing from (or with) our hearts to God, and that singing trains us for godly living. So why is there no mention of Jesus or his word? These verses pretty much parallel Colossians 3:16-17. But where the source of our singing in Colossians is the "word of Christ", here we are filled not with Jesus but with the Holy Spirit. In fact being Spirit-filled is compared to being drunk!

Most likely Paul is trying to show us two sides of the same coin, but with a different emphasis in each passage. So the marks of Spirit-filled Christians include singing to one another and making melody in our hearts to God, whereas word-indwelt Christians teach the truth with gratitude. Both have eyes to each other and to God, but the passages are making different points. The reality is that when we are in Christ, his word dwells in us *and* we are Spirit-filled. We are to sing to build up the church in the gospel *and* we are to sing to offer our heart's response of thanks and praise to God.

One thing we haven't mentioned yet actually ties these passages even more closely together. A possibly more accurate way of translating "psalms and hymns and spiritual songs" is actually to say, "*Spirit-inspired* psalms, hymns and songs".[9] So it's not just the songs that are spiritual but equally the psalms and hymns; in other words, all of our singing! And if the Holy Spirit is leading us to do Spirit-inspired singing in Ephesians, so then is the word of Christ in Colossians. Singing, as much as it is a word ministry, is equally a Spirit activity. One way of thinking about it is that the Holy Spirit 'tunes our hearts to sing thy grace', whereas the word of Christ provides us with the content of that grace. It is not as simple as to say that Colossians 3 is directed towards our minds while Ephesians 5 is aimed our hearts. (Remember, to Paul they are the same thing.) But we can say that word and Spirit work *together*, profoundly affecting the heart, mind, intellect and emotions as we sing—with neither word nor Spirit being effective without the other.

The New Testament singing passages, therefore, help us to understand our singing in terms of a three-way relationship: God ministers his word to us through the work of the Holy Spirit; we take part in that ministry as we sing and teach the word to one another; and we minister to God as we respond with thankfulness—all of which prepares us for works of thankful service.

9 P O'Brien, *The Letter to the Ephesians*, PNTC, Eerdmans, Grand Rapids, 1999, p. 392 (emphasis added).

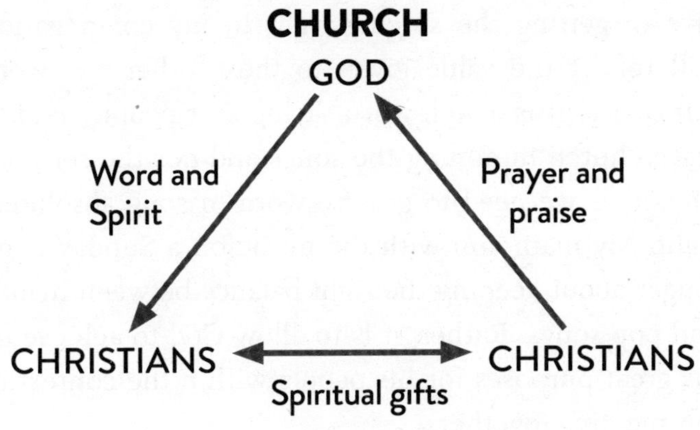

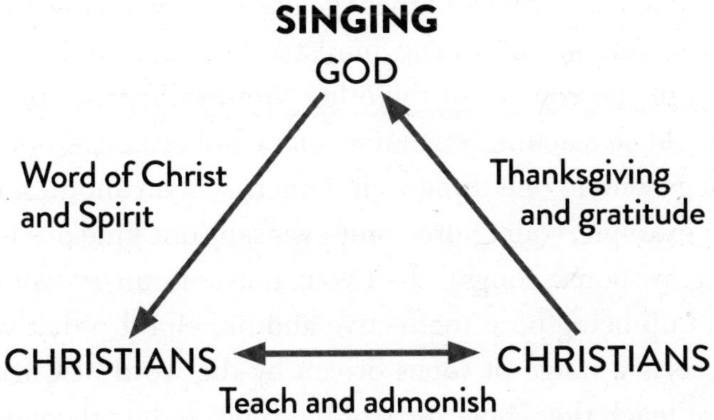

Notice, then, how closely God's purposes for singing mirror his purposes for the church. It's not that singing is merely an application of how church should function. Rather, word-of-Christ singing is a very real and tangible expression of the church living out its purpose in Christ. Therefore, as a music leader or pastor, the weight I give to getting the singing right in my congregation will reflect the value given to those other key word ministries. It is a well-worn saying that people tend to leave church humming the songs and not the sermon! Therefore we need to get the word in song absolutely right. My main aim with the music on a Sunday is no longer about keeping the right balance between hymns and pop songs. Rather, it is to allow God to achieve *all* his great purposes for his people within the context of our meeting together.

Practically, I don't think Paul envisages that each song we sing will achieve all these goals on its own. However, across the whole music ministry of the church, and within the context of the other Word ministries, there should be teaching, encouragement and response. Some songs will do one thing well. Others will do another. If, for example, your church only ever sang one kind of song (e.g. response songs), then your music ministry would end up being both ineffective and unhelpful. What we need is a range of songs driven by the word of Christ that teach the whole story of the Bible and its theology, that reflect our unity with one another in Christ, and that allow us to respond to the gospel with genuine and right emotion. Of course, some songs *are* good at doing more than one thing. Charles Wesley, for example, was brilliant at articulating the truth of the gospel and allowing for an authentic human response:

And can it be that I should gain
An interest in the Saviour's blood![10]

And once the song content is right, we need to give thought to leading our singing (which includes how we accompany it) in a way that most helps our church members to engage with Christ and the church. Unfortunately there is no magic formula for leading music that will work for every church, as each congregation and their musicians will differ in ability, style and culture. But we will speak more of this later.

What the Bible does and doesn't say about singing

Finally, what the Bible doesn't say about singing… is most of those things we desperately want answers for! However, let's remember that our church music issues are, more often than not, quite different from God's. Every time I look at his purposes for our singing, I am amazed at how God uses such a lovely part of his creation to have such an important role in helping us know Jesus and be transformed by him. Yet our concerns are often all too different—like whether we have put in enough hymns in the service to keep the old people happy, or whether we should cut the last song because the sermon has gone on too long, or why can't we find musicians

10 C Wesley, 'And Can It Be, That I Should Gain?', 1738.

to help lead our music. The New Testament rightly does not give us the practical details on how to perform music in church. Our churches would look very odd if we used the same songs, instruments and styles that Paul did! Rather, we are to lead our singing to reflect the profound purposes God has for his people. While the musicians, singers and leaders may get a huge buzz out of leading music in church, their aim should be to first pursue God's goals for our singing—which are all about the word of Christ dwelling in his church, about us exercising our gifts in service of others, and about us responding to him with gratitude in our hearts.

Where we go from here is to think about the content of our singing, and to look at examples from Scripture to determine what a good song looks like—that is, whether it is going to feed, inspire and train our hearts.

3. IF LIFE WERE A MUSICAL...

Musical theatre, be it on the stage or screen, is for me the ultimate experience in escapism. Part of what I enjoy is believing in the unbelievable—when you move from drama to song and back again without thinking how strange that actually is; when a character starts to sing, and the world suddenly changes as the passers-by launch into sophisticated dance routines and begin to sing rich backing harmonies, and the lights and colours become brighter than reality. And then, just as quickly, the song finishes and the story continues as if nothing had happened. But somehow everything has changed...

If you can cope with this concept (and I acknowledge not everyone can), then you are well placed to understand how singing works in the story of the Bible. Perhaps at the end of this chapter you'll no longer feel the need to repress that impulse to simply burst into song. But more importantly, our job here is to understand what it is that God wants from our singing in the church; particularly, how it is that God uses the singing of his word to speak to both the head and heart, in order to shape us for his service. An important question to ask, then, is what should be the content of our songs? Or, more simply, what words should we sing that will allow God to stir our hearts to thankfulness and obedience?

Songs in the Bible

It may or may not come as a surprise to you to find that the Bible is full of songs! Love songs, praise songs, sad songs, repentance songs, teaching songs, prayer songs, and more. And they are not there simply for us to appreciate the ancient use of the ten-stringed harp. The Bible songs, in fact, have a special place in the story of God's plan of salvation for the world. As such, they never occur randomly but nearly always at key times and events. While at first we might not be aware of what is a song and what is not (because we don't have the original Bible soundtrack to help us out), once you figure out what is going on you will notice that the songs are actually linked together with a common thread. They create a sort of song-line—a map of salvation history in singing—that connects the saints of old with us.

a. Salvation signposts

Let's first take a step back and look at the big picture. As you're probably aware, the Bible is not a collection of random ancient writings about God, but is in fact *one* story about how God created us and set about dealing with the issue of our rebellion towards him—ultimately in the death and resurrection of his Son, Jesus Christ. In fact, the Bible only really makes sense when you read it as a whole. But unless you know where you are in the story, things start to get a bit confusing. That's where the Bible songs first become useful. Purely at the literary level, the songs function like signposts to show us where we are in the story. The really good ones not only tell you what has happened up to this point, but help you to make sense of both 'now' and what is about to happen.

So, for example, notice how the period of the Kings is introduced by the song of Hannah in 1 Samuel 2. It starts as a song of personal thanks (when God grants her request for a child):

> "My heart exults in the LORD;
>   my horn is exalted in the LORD.
> My mouth derides my enemies,
>   because I rejoice in your salvation." (v. 1)

Then it moves to expounding God's faithfulness to his people, and ultimately foretelling his purposes for establishing a king:

"The adversaries of the LORD shall be broken to
pieces;
against them he will thunder in heaven.
The LORD will judge the ends of the earth;
he will give strength to his king
and exalt the horn of his anointed." (v. 10)

Similarly, notice how in Luke 1, Mary sings of God's never-ending faithfulness to her and his people, preparing us for the new kingdom to arrive in Jesus Christ:

"And his mercy is for those who fear him
from generation to generation...
He has helped his servant Israel,
in remembrance of his mercy,
as he spoke to our fathers,
to Abraham and to his offspring forever."
(vv. 50, 54-55)

And then look to the end of biblical history, as the saints gather around the heavenly throne in Revelation 5:

And they sang a new song, saying,

"Worthy are you to take the scroll
and to open its seals,
for you were slain, and by your blood you
ransomed people for God
from every tribe and language and people
and nation,

and you have made them a kingdom and
priests to our God,
and they shall reign on the earth."
(vv. 9-10)

The theme of each song is essentially the same: that God is faithful in keeping his promises, and is powerful to save. And each song is a signpost, pointing us towards the greatest of all acts of salvation: to Christ, whether that be in past redemption or our future glory.

b. Emotional cues

We all know something of how music can act as a cue to what we are meant to feel. It wasn't long into the development of cinema that movie makers realized they could use music to create a whole new layer of emotional experience in a film. And that was still in the era of silent films! Today, more than ever, movies will use all the colours and textures of the orchestra (as well as lots of electronic wizardry) to give us cues to exactly what we should be feeling at any point in the story. It is many years since I saw the film *The Mission*, but I can still vividly recall the music and emotion of the climactic scene as the gentle oboe melody jars with the violence and destruction of the film's conclusion. Emotional cues can be very powerful.

So it is with the songs in the Bible. As we have said, singing takes place at all the big moments in the story of salvation. But more importantly, these songs find their real purpose within their actual context, because God works his purposes out in the lives of real people—be they kings or lepers—with real longings, hurts, fears, aspirations and dreams. These songs tell us both what we need to *know* about God's plan and what we are meant to *feel* as God interacts with us.

Remember the song in the musical? What was not evident in the action of the story is revealed as the song unpacks the thoughts and feelings of the character singing it. The song emotionally interprets the world and circumstances around them—which is very similar to the songs and poems we find in Scripture. In the big picture of God's story, songs help us know where we are going. But up close they show us the right and real emotional response to God's actions and purposes in the world.

So, for example, let's look back at one big day in the life of Israel: the day when God redeemed his people by bringing them out of slavery in Egypt. It was an extraordinary rescue and involved the use of powerful signs and wonders, destroying the pursuing Egyptian army, and leading the people of Israel on in safety to the other side of the Red Sea. What is the first thing Israel does? What is the first act of the newly saved people of God? They sing!

> "I will sing to the Lord, for he has triumphed
> gloriously;
> the horse and his rider he has thrown into the
> sea.

> The LORD is my strength and my song,
> and he has become my salvation;
> this is my God, and I will praise him,
> my father's God, and I will exalt him."
> (Exod 15:1-2)

Before they get caught up in the practicalities of their new life of freedom—such as 'Where are we going?' and 'What are we going to eat?'—the Israelites do the absolutely most appropriate thing they could possibly do: they respond to God's salvation in thanks and praise. Yes, they soon *do* get caught up in the practicalities of their new life. But their first response is completely right: to thank God. The fact that they sang shows that the response was genuine, heartfelt and appropriately emotional. And what Israel did on that first day was to set up a pattern of singing in response to the saving work of God—a response that firstly recalls what God has done, but equally a response that allows the singer to express godly emotions; emotions that are stirred when we receive and remember God's saving grace.

c. Psalms

It would be hard to speak of the songs of the Bible, and particularly those that express genuine emotion, without saying something of the book of Psalms. Of course, there is no way in this short space to do justice to the complexity and richness of the material in this collection of songs. It is clear that the psalms were central to the public praise of Israel, and the book of Psalms was very likely held up to be one of, if not *the* key hymnbook of the early church. That they are specifically mentioned and commanded in Colossians 3 and Ephesians 5 shows that Paul thought them essential to the right expression of faith within the Christian church.

What the psalms offer us is undoubted. Nowhere else in Scripture is there such depth and variety of expression of emotion within the context of salvation and grace. But, more incredibly, the psalms are songs about Jesus—and songs sung *by* Jesus:

> My God, my God, why have you forsaken me?
> Why are you so far from saving me, from the words of my groaning?
> O my God, I cry by day, but you do not answer,
> and by night, but I find no rest.
> Yet you are holy,
> enthroned on the praises of Israel.
> In you our fathers trusted;
> they trusted, and you delivered them.
> To you they cried and were rescued;
> in you they trusted and were not put to shame.
> (Ps 22:1-5)

> Now from the sixth hour there was darkness over all the land until the ninth hour. And about the ninth hour Jesus cried out with a loud voice, saying, "Eli, Eli, lema sabachthani?" that is, "My God, my God, why have you forsaken me?" (Matt 27:45-46)

It is amazing to think that at the cross—the climactic moment in salvation history where Christ is enduring the wrath of God for our sins—he would sing to himself this song. How astounding that in the darkest moment of his life, and indeed of human history, he would sing into his soul a reminder of God's holiness, faithfulness and saving power; that he could sing of his own death in terms of bringing perfect praise to the Father. These are complex emotions for any song, and yet how apt they are when spoken by Jesus at his death; and how mind blowing that they were written hundreds of years before, for that very purpose.

It may not be that we can so easily own the words to psalms such as this. But I would suggest that within the book of Psalms you will find each and every shade of emotion that reflects and makes sense of life, faith and salvation—and in ways that model to us what godly singing looks like.

Here are just a few examples.

Pure adoration

O Lord, our Lord,
how majestic is your name in all the earth! (8:1)

Spiritual despair

How long, O Lord? Will you forget me forever?
How long will you hide your face from me?
How long must I take counsel in my soul
and have sorrow in my heart all the day? (13:1-2)

Comfort in the face of death

Even though I walk through the valley of the
shadow of death,
I will fear no evil,
for you are with me;
your rod and your staff,
they comfort me. (23:4)

Praise for the God who rescues

I waited patiently for the LORD;
he inclined to me and heard my cry.
He drew me up from the pit of destruction,
out of the miry bog,
and set my feet upon a rock,
making my steps secure.
He put a new song in my mouth,
a song of praise to our God. (40:1-3)

The sinner's cry for mercy

Have mercy on me, O God,
according to your steadfast love;
according to your abundant mercy
blot out my transgressions.
Wash me thoroughly from my iniquity,
and cleanse me from my sin! (51:1-2)

God: our only security and satisfaction

Whom have I in heaven but you?

And there is nothing on earth that I desire
besides you.
My flesh and my heart may fail,
but God is the strength of my heart and my
portion forever. (73:25-26)

The longing to be in God's presence

How lovely is your dwelling place,
O LORD of hosts!
My soul longs, yes, faints
for the courts of the LORD;
my heart and flesh sing for joy
to the living God. (84:1-2)

Singing about singing

It is good to give thanks to the LORD,
to sing praises to your name, O Most High;
to declare your steadfast love in the morning,
and your faithfulness by night,
to the music of the lute and the harp,
to the melody of the lyre.
For you, O LORD, have made me glad by your work;
at the works of your hands I sing for joy. (92:1-4)

Joy in knowing the steadfast love of our Father God

Make a joyful noise to the LORD, all the earth!
Serve the LORD with gladness!
Come into his presence with singing!

Know that the LORD, he is God!
It is he who made us, and we are his;
we are his people, and the sheep of his pasture.

Enter his gates with thanksgiving,
and his courts with praise!
Give thanks to him; bless his name!

For the LORD is good;
his steadfast love endures forever,
and his faithfulness to all generations. (100:1-5)

The blessings of the Lord

Blessed is everyone who fears the LORD,
who walks in his ways!
You shall eat the fruit of the labor of your hands;
you shall be blessed, and it shall be well with
you. (128:1-2)

The how and why of praise

Praise the LORD!
Praise God in his sanctuary;
praise him in his mighty heavens!
Praise him for his mighty deeds;
praise him according to his excellent greatness!

Praise him with trumpet sound;
praise him with lute and harp!
Praise him with tambourine and dance;
praise him with strings and pipe!

Praise him with sounding cymbals;
    praise him with loud clashing cymbals!
Let everything that has breath praise the LORD!
Praise the LORD! (150:1-6)

So how do the Bible songs guide us in what we should sing? Well, they always teach something about God—nearly always about his faithfulness and saving works, and a lot about his character. And they also touch the heart, as the singer is forced to respond with right and genuine emotion to God's acts of grace—whether that be with tears or laughter.

Praise

Even the briefest look at the Bible songs will highlight how significant the idea of 'praise' is. And as with 'worship', praise is a concept that we regularly connect with our own singing—to the extent that today we have a 'Praise and Worship' industry, a massive global business of writing and publishing Christian congregational music. But while we have seen that the 'worship song' doesn't really exist in biblical thinking, Scripture *does* talk about songs of praise. Psalm 22:3, for instance, describes God as enthroned on Israel's songs of praise (*tehilla*). Does that mean, then, that praise is actually the right term to describe our singing? Well, again—not really!

Clearly, singing is a great vehicle for praise. But praise itself is a far bigger idea than a joyful song.

a. Hallelujah

Hallelujah is literally a call to praise Yahweh, or "Praise the Lord!" This word bookends Psalm 150 (which we just saw above)—a psalm that explains where to praise him, when to praise him, how to praise him and who should praise him. But while it would be easy to think that singing the psalm is itself the act of praise, if anything the psalm calls us to appreciate a far bigger picture of what God expects. 'Praise' declares how great and excellent God is, and the things he has done which demonstrate that greatness. And praise is demanded of all creation, in heaven as much as on earth. Of course, in its very nature praise is not sombre or performed grudgingly, but is done with all the fervour and excitement of playing in the most magnificent orchestra.

It is in heaven itself that we hear the perfect declaration of the praise of the redeemed:

> After this I heard what seemed to be the loud voice of a great multitude in heaven, crying out,
>
> "Hallelujah!
> Salvation and glory and power belong to our God,
> for his judgements are true and just..."
> (Rev 19:1-2)

If praise is about proclaiming what God has done, then there is no greater truth to declare than the gospel itself. God deserves glory because he alone has brought an end to sin through Christ's magnificent victory over death at the cross.

b. God brings praise to himself

It is not just human words that bring God praise. God's creation similarly declares his glory *to* the creation:

> The heavens declare the glory of God,
> and the sky above proclaims his handiwork.
> Day to day pours out speech,
> and night to night reveals knowledge.
> There is no speech, nor are there words,
> whose voice is not heard. (Ps 19:1-3)

However, and ultimately, it is God's greatest work that brings him the greatest praise. Paul, in Ephesians 1, cannot describe our union with Christ without pausing at every step to let God bring praise to himself:

> ...In love he predestined us for adoption as sons through Jesus Christ, according to the purpose of his will, to the praise of his glorious grace, with which he has blessed us in the Beloved. (Eph 1:4-6)

The revelation of this profound mystery leads him three times to describe our adoption as God's children as being "to the praise of his glory" (vv. 6, 12, 14)!

c. Praise in the life of faith

> In this you rejoice, though now for a little while, if necessary, you have been grieved by various trials, so that the tested genuineness of your faith—more precious than gold that perishes though it is tested by fire—may be found to result in praise and glory and honour at the revelation of Jesus Christ. (1 Pet 1:6-7)

Praise is also the result of the life lived by faith. In particular, it is our endurance in life's trials that gives us cause to rejoice, knowing that at the end of all things Jesus will be honoured and glorified through his refining work in us. We will see later that it is not the 'successful' Christian life that will generate praise in our singing. No, just as love flows from sacrifice and joy from judgement, praise is founded on the hope of glory.

Think back to our discussion about worship, and remember that the *service* God demands of us is not what makes us right with him, but is the lived-out response of those who are saved by grace. Praise is part of that service—whether spoken, sung or lived out in faith. So 'praise' doesn't simply equal 'singing'. But just as singing the word of Christ helps us to engage our hearts with the gospel, so too the Bible's call for us to *sing* praise reminds us that praise is an action of the heart—that declaring the great things of God can only ever be done out of genuine joy. And while we may not always have a loud cymbal to hand, the business of praising is as fundamental to the life of the Christian as eating and drinking.

Singing in all of life

So too, it seems, is singing. Now it may be stating the obvious, but none of the examples of singing we have seen in Scripture have been within the walls of a church. Yes, the psalms may have been used as a hymnbook in the temple. But many of those were written (and sung) amidst the ordinary and extraordinary circumstances of life. Songs are sung by those in humble submission, in the exhilaration of victory, the fear of death, the joy of community, the darkness of prison, and in awe of God's saving power. So, while it is vital for us to figure out how singing should work in our churches, the Bible (even in the New Testament) does not restrict our song to the gathered assembly. Practically, some songs in their content and music will particularly suit a congregational setting—indeed, the gathered church seems to be the place where singing best fulfils God's purposes for the word in song. But as a vehicle for the heart to be taught and to respond to the word, singing is never restricted to Sundays. This is why James can say, "Is anyone among you suffering? Let him pray. Is anyone cheerful? Let him sing praise" (Jas 5:13). The example of the character in the musical spontaneously bursting into song is not so strange when you remember that in Scripture

God touches hearts with the song of his grace in every moment and circumstance of life.

Songs ancient and modern

So how then do we fit together the New Testament's teaching on singing with what we see in the Bible's own songs? Well, the pattern of recalling God's work followed by the heart's response is exactly what is described in Colossians 3:16-17. In the Bible songs, God speaks his word to the heart in order that the singer would speak that word to others and return it to God in praise. The Bible songs show us what the gospel word looks like in real life. They show us that the Word is not only the essential content of our songs; it is also the means of the Holy Spirit in effecting his radical work in us. God uses his word to rule, accomplishing his will in creation and in our lives. God's word is not just information *about* God, but it is how he engages with us, both in the person of Christ and in the Scriptures:

> All Scripture is breathed out by God and profitable for teaching, for reproof, for correction, and for training in righteousness, that the man of God may be complete, equipped for every good work. (2 Tim 3:16-17)

Notice the power of the Word as we receive and respond to it. No part of life and ministry is untouched by it. It teaches us. It corrects us. It weakens sin by shining a spotlight into the darkness of our hearts. And it trains us in righteousness for the life of thankful obedience as we read it, and hear it, and sing it!

How well, then, do your song choices live up to those in Scripture? Do they have that same focus on the faithfulness and saving power of God—salvation that demands a response of heartfelt thanks and obedience? How well do your songs point to Christ and the gospel as the centre of history, and life, and faith?

It seems that within every great movement in the history of the church there has been a new approach to singing and, in particular, what we sing. During the Reformation, for instance, you had Calvin stating that we should only sing the songs actually recorded in Scripture (i.e. let the Bible do all the work in deciding song content); while Luther began writing his own hymns based on Bible texts and themes; while Zwingli demanded that there be no singing at all! Then, during the evangelical revival, Isaac Watts began writing hymns to reinterpret the psalms to point to Christ, at the same time as Charles Wesley sought to emphasize salvation and our heart's response:

> My chains fell off, my heart was free,
> I rose, went forth, and followed thee.[11]

Recent years, of course, have seen a proliferation of new songs. While many of these will reflect the biblical

11 'And Can It Be, That I Should Gain?'

models we have described, others (as has always been the case) will tend to reflect worldly ideas and aspirations. An issue for today's church is that songs can often be so individualistic that they actually work against the mutual encouragement of our brothers and sisters. Or what about churches that promote a mystical view of faith? How many songs do we come across that speak of what I am going to do for God—rather than what he has done for us? Or what about churches that promote moral teaching over the gospel? How many Christian songs could otherwise be secular pop songs with Jesus being a substitute for my boy/girlfriend, but without any basis in biblical doctrine? We must never let go of the truth that the gospel word is powerful to teach, correct and train us in righteousness, equipping us for every good work. That's why the word of Christ should be at the heart of every song we sing—whatever century we have taken it from or whatever musical style we employ.

So our songs needn't all look and sound the same. Remember the phrase "Spirit-inspired psalms, hymns and songs" (Colossians 3 and Ephesians 5)? I think there is a clue here that song choices can and should be diverse in style and content. Governed by the word of Christ, prayer, praise, confession, encouragement and teaching are all things we should be singing about—not to mention the many other themes that can be brought into those genres.

Our rule should always be that whatever the song, we apply the same criteria to it as we would to any other expression of word ministry: Is it true? Is it clear? Is it rich in Scripture? Does it make sense of the biblical context? Is the application appropriate? Does it apply the gospel to the heart? And so on. In this way, our preaching and singing should wonderfully complement each other—the same message, aimed at mind and heart, in order to move the listeners towards faithful, thankful obedience to Christ.

Summary

The Bible songs connect the truths and purposes of God with the singer's heart-response to those truths. They are an intersection of theology and emotional engagement. Importantly, Bible songs model what we should be singing about: our salvation (ultimately in the cross of Christ), and our thankful response to being saved by God's grace.

So the Bible makes it clear that the content of our singing is to be the gospel, the word of Christ. It is also clear that this is a ministry that occurs profoundly at the level of the heart. But what is not so clear is how the heart is affected as we sing that word, and what it is that we should be feeling. How can we be confident it is the gospel at work in us as we sing, and not just random emotions? These are the issues of the next chapter.

4. I FEEL GOOD: MUSIC AND EMOTION

I have a love/hate relationship with running. I love the idea of it, because I see the health benefits. It allows me to eat more cake, and keeps my brain working. On the other hand, it hurts! I sort of feel conned by all those veteran runners who led me to believe that at a certain point a release of endorphins would magically take away all the pain and send me into a callisthenically induced high. I have never felt such a thing. It always just hurts.

This is a good example of how we are not all the same in the way we respond to things. Many Christians, for example, have been taught to express emotions in a particular way, and so they feel uneasy every time they go to their church meeting. They question themselves about why they feel so passionately about something that others appear unmoved by. Singing is one of those occasions when we are forced to nail our colours to the mast—because very rarely do you find a church where there is not some unspoken rule on the correct way to express the things you are feeling, particularly in the singing. To do something different means risking being quietly assessed for your theological (and emotional) soundness.

Most of us listen to music because we want it to stir our feelings. So we use music to amplify the things we are already experiencing—to help us feel sorrow more deeply or to intensify our joy. And different styles of music will do that for different people. Some will find very little connection with music, while others are transported into another world when they listen to something they love. We are not all the same, but we all do feel *something* when music engages us.

Singing, however, takes musical engagement a step further. Whereas listening to music is a passive experience, singing requires a physical connection. It is why many people will join a choir or musical theatre group, or will sing along loudly to whatever they're listening to in the car—for the satisfaction of actually engaging in the music. The Bible looks at music in a very similar way. While we might think about music as an artistic endeavour (or something we admire from a distance), God sees our singing as something we participate in—as a physical *and* spiritual activity. It is not something we observe, but something we do:

> Clap your hands, all peoples!
>   Shout to God with loud songs of joy!

> For the LORD, the Most High, is to be feared,
> a great king over all the earth. (Ps 47:1-2)

And as the Bible so clearly connects singing, the gospel, and the human heart, it is right then that we also look to the Bible to understand our emotions and how to express them appropriately. Getting emotion wrong can easily destroy authenticity in our gatherings. It can lead to dissatisfaction and spiritual confusion; or to mysticism, where our feelings outweigh our confidence in God's grace. On the other hand, getting emotion right will make the church gathering one of the most genuine and encouraging experiences in the Christian life, as together our hearts are opened to the transformative power of the Word and Spirit.

We started this book by asking where singing fits in the Christian experience. And we've seen that the longings of the empty heart can never find satisfaction in idolatry (worship of music, relationships, money, sex, affirmation, family, etc.) but only in true worship: the state of a restored heart in union with Christ. Singing can't get us to God. It can't replace true worship in Christ. But it is nonetheless a 'heart thing'. As we have seen, it connects Christ, the Holy Spirit, and the gospel with our hearts in a profound way that challenges how we then live our lives.

Of course, talking about emotion within church and church music is not without danger! Because of our different church backgrounds, theological viewpoints, musical interests, and often simply because of the way we are individually wired, we can bring a lot of baggage to this issue. When it comes to figuring out what authentic expression of emotion in church should look like, we can still end up holding vastly different opinions about what is genuine, what is appropriate, and what it is exactly that God wants us to do with our feelings.

Just so we are clear, this chapter is not about criticizing or promoting any particular style of doing church. I have never found the perfect church, and don't expect to till I enter the heavenly assembly. I am guessing that you will already have some views on these issues—perhaps you are concerned that either thinking or feeling is done to excess in your church, or is out of balance; or perhaps you feel guilty that you lean one way when the rest of your church leans the other. What I want us to be clear about is that the gospel *should* affect our feelings, emotions, thoughts and actions. Yes, it is easy for us to criticize others who either *think* too much or *feel* too much. But I would like us to let the Scriptures critique these things first. Like preaching, singing the Word is a ministry that requires us to engage our hearts and our minds with Jesus, in humility and submission, in order to faithfully serve him and his church.

Emotion in Christian experience

a. Facts, faith, feelings

There is a commonly held position in some churches that

says feelings are untrustworthy in the Christian life. One example is the slogan 'Facts, Faith, Feelings' (FFF), which encapsulates the idea that faith is built upon the facts of the gospel, which in turn may or may not then lead to any feelings about our salvation. The idea is that while facts and faith are reliable, feelings are not. I guess the slogan helps guard against the idea that genuine conversion needs to include a mystical 'spiritual' experience; and protects us from bypassing God's word when it comes to understanding his will for our lives.

However, while those dangers are very real, this position has some fundamental flaws.

Firstly, it discounts all the *other* language in the New Testament around the *experience* of conversion and living for Christ. Emotions are never discounted—no matter where one stands with God. Paul, for example, contrasts the emotions of our pre-conversion life (anger, hate, rage, envy, etc.) with those tied to knowing Christ (joy, hope, peace, etc.). In doing so he ties our emotions to salvation, as evidence of the supernaturally transformed heart.

Secondly, I think FFF unfairly downplays the place and purpose of God-inspired emotion. Of course the Bible never says that our feelings should be the primary guide in faith and Christian living. However, it does describe the goal of our faith in emotional terms:

> Therefore, since we have been justified by faith, we have peace with God through our Lord Jesus Christ. Through him we have also obtained access

> by faith into this grace in which we stand, and we rejoice in hope of the glory of God. (Rom 5:1-2)

Here, Paul says that faith is not an end in itself, but has a higher purpose—to bring us to *peace* with God, thereby giving us grounds to *rejoice* in the *hope* of God's glory. This joy (and hope, for that matter) is not an optional extra. It is our goal. Joy is where facts and faith drive us. The gospel moves us from being God's enemies through faith to being those who are at peace and full of joy in him.

FFF has a valid point to make: that true faith is not founded on how we feel about God. Its flaw, however, is in how it describes life with God—without much life in it.

b. Jonathan Edwards

One alternative view says that emotions are *essential* in conversion and faith:

> How can they [i.e. those gathered in church] sit and hear of the infinite height, and depth, and length, and breadth of the love of God in Christ Jesus… manifested in His dying agonies, His bloody sweat, His loud and bitter cries, and bleeding heart, and all this for enemies, to redeem them from deserved, eternal burnings, and to bring to unspeakable and everlasting joy and glory—and yet be cold and heavy, insensible and regardless![12]

12 J Edwards, *A Treatise on the Religious Affections*, Banner of Truth, Edinburgh, 1986 [1746], p. 52.

These words were written by Jonathan Edwards, a Presbyterian minister in North America during a period of great revival in the 18th century. He wrote in opposition to those who criticized the emotionalism of that revival. Edwards admitted that emotions on their own were not enough to establish authentic conversion. But he did try to defend the great outpouring of emotion that was going on by pointing to the fact that many lives were being genuinely changed.

He did this in a book called *The Religious Affections*. Affections are things within us (including our emotions and thoughts) that are directed towards something external—for instance, God. (So being 'affectionate' is not just a feeling of love but also an expression of that feeling.) When the Holy Spirit is at work in our lives, he transforms us in order that we might respond with affection towards God. These 'religious affections' are the emotional and intellectual drivers of our actions. A good example of God stirring our affections is the fruit of the Spirit in Galatians 5, which starts with the chief affection: love.[13]

For Edwards, affections were essential to true religion—but they had to be tested. The test was whether you lived a

13 Edwards wrote that true religion resides in the heart (the seat of affections, or emotions), and he came up with 12 'marks' or indicators to determine the presence of true religion. The first of these was a religious affection arising "from those influences and operations on the heart, which are spiritual, supernatural and divine" (ibid., p. 264). In other words, emotions affected by God (i.e. not the emotion we feel when we drop a brick on our foot) *can* be an indication of faith.

godly life. So, for example, if you were to passionately sing, "I love you, Lord" in church on Sunday, and yet go out and live a life of deliberate sin the next day, it would suggest that no matter what you felt when you were singing, it was not likely to have been a 'religious affection'.

As with FFF, Edwards has helpful points to make in how we understand emotion in the Christian life. But there is in fact a bigger picture the Bible paints on this issue—that our emotions are derived first from God's own character; and that in Christ, our emotions have an essential role to play in how we experience salvation in its fullness.

Emotion in Christian singing

Edwards was of course quick to point out the connection between the affections and singing:

> The duty of singing praises to God, seems to be appointed wholly to excite and express religious affections. No other reason can be assigned, why we should express ourselves to God in verse, rather than in prose, and do it with music, but only, that such is our nature and frame, that these things have a tendency to move our affections.[14]

In other words (and it may be stating the obvious!), we sing praise rather than speak it precisely because it *does*

14 Edwards, op. cit., p. 34.

stir our emotions. But if that is the case, doesn't it mean that we should be actively pursuing emotion in our church's music? Shouldn't we, through our singing, be chasing that inexpressible joy which is the outcome of our faith? Here are two responses to this question.

a. Martin Luther

> For whether you wish to comfort the sad, to terrify the happy, to encourage the despairing, to humble the proud, to calm the passionate, or to appease those full of hate… what more effective means than music could you find?… [Music] is a mistress and governess of those human emotions.[15]

These are the words of Martin Luther, the first great Protestant Reformer and a musician and composer at that. Encouraging both popular and 'art' music in his churches, he was passionate about music for its emotive qualities. However, he understood that the emotions that arise during singing should be *generated by God's word*—not by the way the music is played. For Luther, music was foremost a vehicle for the proclamation of the word of God:

> The gift of language combined with the gift of song was only given to man to let him know that

15 M Luther, 'Preface to Georg Rhau's Symphoniae iucundae', trans. US Leupold, 1538, in J Pelikan and HT Lehmann (eds), *Luther's Works*, vol. 53, *Liturgy and Hymns*, ed. US Leupold, Fortress, Philadelphia, 1965, p. 323.

> he should praise God with both word and music, namely, by proclaiming [God's word] through music and by providing sweet melodies with words.[16]

Luther's hymns, therefore, show a commitment to teaching scriptural truth, but they also encourage us to submit our emotions to that truth as they are shaped and driven by the gospel at work in us:

> And though this world, with devils filled,
> should threaten to undo us,
> We will not fear, for God hath willed
> His truth to triumph through us.[17]

Similarly, the emotions find their source not in us but in God. He effects praise in us in order that we might deliver it back to him:

> All this for us Thy love hath done;
> By this to Thee our love is won;
> For this our joyful songs we raise,
> For this we sing Thee ceaseless praise.[18]

Luther was committed to the word of God; he advocated music as a means for proclaiming the word of God; and he was positive about emotion in music—as long as it was shaped by the word of God. If Luther had concerns

16 Luther, ibid., p. 321.
17 M Luther, 'A Mighty Fortress is Our God', trans. FH Hedge, 1853 [1529].
18 M Luther, 'All Praise to Thee, Eternal Lord', 1524; trans. unknown, 1858.

about emotionalism in church music, they were to do with letting the music drive the experience, over the gospel. I suspect he was reacting not to the local mega-church down the road so much as to the mysticism he saw within Roman Catholicism. A contemporary example of this would be what we see happening in some forms of charismaticism.

b. Pentecostalism

One of the standout features of modern charismatic churches is their well-performed and passionate singing. One reason I have heard for this is that charismatic Christians are more emotionally expressive people than others in the Christian community! While that may be true to some extent, I think there are more fundamental theological reasons as to why music is so important for some churches—particularly those influenced by the Pentecostal movement. It comes down to the idea that experiencing emotion can be evidence of knowing the immanent blessings of God, or a sign of being filled with the Holy Spirit. Pentecostalism is essentially Arminian—that is, it sees the things *we do* as being what makes the blessings of God possible. Therefore it makes sense to work hard on making great music in order to evoke strong emotions, because it satisfies God's demands for 'our worship' and in return he guarantees the experience of his blessing.

So, for example (and this is huge generalization!), in the Pentecostal tradition you are more likely to sing a song that says, "I love you God and am going to do this for you", than one that says, "God, you have loved me, and I thank you for it". Of course, it's never going to be that black and white. The basic facts of the gospel will be true in most Christian songs, whatever their origin. What is important in assessing any song is not just whether it proclaims the gospel, but also whether it adds to it or leaves something out.

So in churches that preach a prosperity gospel, you might notice a tendency for songs to be triumphalistic: they might be essentially true (in describing God's power to bless), but they will lack any sorrow for our sin or the state of our need for forgiveness. And chances are they will ignore the New Testament's teaching that genuine blessing is a promise guaranteed only for the new creation.

Or in over-emphasizing 'old covenant worship', a church may allow its songs to dwell on temple and sacrifice language, missing Christ's glorious fulfillment of Old Testament worship. Its songs will aim to mystically fan the fire of our emotional engagement with God. Of course, when the emphasis is on meeting God in 'his house', you are in danger of missing out on encountering God's grace in Christ.

What we are questioning here is not a genuineness of love for Christ or a passion for singing about it, but a theology of worship that is based on a mystical engagement with God, or which borrows the language of the Old Testament to give it biblical credibility. It is not at all wrong to feel the emotion tied to knowing Christ.

We are designed to long for that! The thing to remember, however, is that there is nothing our music and singing can do to get us any nearer to Christ; we are not nearer to Christ because we feel a particular way when we sing. In Jesus, God is and always has been with us—perfectly.

Emotion in the Bible

So let's think a bit more then about what the Bible has to say about emotion in church and, in turn, in our music. To help us, we will be aiming to answer these two questions:

a. How does the Bible describe emotion within God himself?
b. What emotions should be evident in the church?

a. Emotion within God

As we are created in God's likeness, and because we are emotional beings, it follows that the Bible shows God our creator to be equally full of emotion. However, that is where the similarities end! For God experiences emotion most perfectly *within himself*—within the Trinity of Father, Son and Holy Spirit, the divine relationships which exist perfectly from and into eternity. As there are many books written on just this topic, we are not going to spend time here unpacking the doctrine of the Trinity. What we will do, however, is think briefly about two emotions of God—love and joy—and how they affect us as his image bearers and the church.

The love of the Father and the Son

We first witness the love of the Father as he speaks to the Son in whom he delights:

> He was still speaking when, behold, a bright cloud overshadowed them, and a voice from the cloud said, "This is my beloved Son, with whom I am well pleased; listen to him". (Matt 17:5)

We all know what it feels like to be loved and affirmed. And we have all seen the glowing face of a child who has been praised and encouraged. I think that Jesus, too, must have taken great delight in his Father's public praise of him. Theirs is a relationship not of cold command and obedience, but of deep, rich and transforming affection.

Of course, as saved sinners, *we* first of all engage with the love of God through the sacrifice of his Son:

> In this is love, not that we have loved God but that he loved us and sent his Son to be the propitiation for our sins. (1 John 4:10)

And as Christ's body, the church is to reflect the love of God:

> "As the Father has loved me, so have I loved you. Abide in my love." (John 15:9)

This love (surpassing even faith and hope) is to establish and fill the relationships of the church:

> Love is patient and kind; love does not envy or boast; it is not arrogant or rude. It does not insist on its own way; it is not irritable or resentful; it does not rejoice at wrongdoing, but rejoices with the truth. Love bears all things, believes all things, hopes all things, endures all things. (1 Cor 13:4-7)

And revisiting Romans 12, we see that love tops the list of applications illustrating what it means to offer our bodies as living sacrifices:

> Let love be genuine. Abhor what is evil; hold fast to what is good. Love one another with brotherly affection. Outdo one another in showing honour. (Rom 12:9-10)

The joy of the Father and the Son

Closely tied to love is joy, the emotion that fills the act of rejoicing. Looking towards the future restored Israel, God says "he will joy over thee with singing" (Zeph 3:17, KJV). Though it will cost God dearly to pour out his wrath in judgement on his people Israel, towards those who he chooses to save he cannot but rejoice and delight.

And then of Jesus we read:

> ...let us run with endurance the race that is set before us, looking to Jesus, the founder and perfecter of our faith, who for the joy that was

> set before him endured the cross, despising the shame, and is seated at the right hand of the throne of God. (Heb 12:1-3)

This passage describes Jesus as the one who ultimately endures God's wrath, and who therefore is the means by which God saves. But what is extraordinary is that Jesus' goal in death is the pursuit of joy! Not, I think, a joy in experiencing suffering, but a joy in the delight of doing his father's pleasure, in establishing the very kingdom over which he now rules and to which we now belong. That kingdom is itself characterized by joy:

> For the kingdom of God is not a matter of eating and drinking but of righteousness and peace and joy in the Holy Spirit. (Rom 14:17)

The emotions of God are vast, unmeasured and boundless. Love and joy, however, reveal to us the heart of his character. God lavishes his love upon us, and joy fills all those who are willing to trust and obey him. The fact that love flows from sacrifice, and joy flows from judgement, shows that such affection is profoundly supernatural, and not in the same category as worldly pleasure and infatuation (as nice as they can feel).

Of course, God shows many other emotions towards his creation, such as grief, anger, sorrow and compassion. But within the Trinity and towards his own children, love and joy abound.

b. Emotion within the church

If love and joy are central to God's character, it is no wonder that the Bible again and again describes those emotions as foundational for our own attitudes towards God and each other:

> Though you have not seen him, you love him. Though you do not now see him, you believe in him and rejoice with joy that is inexpressible and filled with glory… (1 Pet 1:8)

> So if there is any encouragement in Christ, any comfort from love, any participation in the Spirit, any affection and sympathy, complete my joy by being of the same mind, having the same love, being in full accord and of one mind. (Phil 2:1-3)

> But the fruit of the Spirit is love, joy, peace, patience, kindness, goodness, faithfulness… (Gal 5:22)

The Bible overflows with love and joy—deep affections that extend between us and God and each other. But our whole experience of life and faith, with its sufferings and trials, makes sense only when we remember that God first poured his love into our hearts:

> Therefore, since we have been justified by faith, we have peace with God through our Lord Jesus Christ. Through him we have also obtained access by faith into this grace in which we stand, and we

> rejoice in hope of the glory of God. Not only that, but we rejoice in our sufferings, knowing that suffering produces endurance, and endurance produces character, and character produces hope, and hope does not put us to shame, because God's love has been poured into our hearts through the Holy Spirit who has been given to us. (Rom 5:1-5)

What is important to point out here is that love and joy won't always equate to what we consider 'normal' experiences of emotion. They are much more profound; much deeper than the simple pleasures you might have from meeting with a good friend, falling in love or listening to a great piece of music, as nice as those things are. The Bible shows us joy in sorrow as well as in gladness. That is why David can cry out from the depths of anguish yet still have an unshakable hope in the Lord (Psalm 130). It is why Paul and Silas could sing hymns while locked in the filthy Philippian jail (Acts 16). Real joy is both knowing in our heads that we are loved by God, and being able to delight in him in our souls.

By the waters of Babylon: the emotions of the broken heart

I think it is fair to say that, on the whole, Christians are good at singing about the love of God and the joy of salvation. There is one category of emotion, however, that is not hugely popular in contemporary Christian music: that associated with our brokenness and sin.

And while the clear trajectory of Scripture *is* pushing us towards experiencing the 'exalted emotions' (joy, peace, etc.) of our new life in Christ, it never ignores the reality of living in this fallen world and the ongoing struggles we have with sorrow, despair and guilt.

The lament, or song of grief, for instance, is a significant theme in the book of Psalms. It is the song sung by those who feel far away from God, but who nonetheless trust in his faithfulness:

Awake! Why are you sleeping, O Lord?
Rouse yourself! Do not reject us forever!
Why do you hide your face?
Why do you forget our affliction and oppression?
For our soul is bowed down to the dust;
our belly clings to the ground.
Rise up; come to our help!
Redeem us for the sake of your steadfast love!
(Ps 44:23-26)

Also significant is the confession, the words of a sinner humbly seeking for God's forgiveness:

For I know my transgressions,
and my sin is ever before me.
Against you, you only, have I sinned
and done what is evil in your sight,
so that you may be justified in your words
and blameless in your judgement. (Ps 51:3-4)

Such songs help make sense of the uncertainty, fragility and pain of this life. The Bible's 'sorrowful songs' allow the singer to articulate the very real emotions of life in the fallen creation. But at the same time they never doubt God's sovereignty and justice; and never discount our own responsibility in sin.

The thankful heart of the redeemed

There is one other key emotion that we need to take note of, which is special to *us* as God's rescued people, and that is *thankfulness*:[19]

> Let the word of Christ dwell in you richly, teaching and admonishing one another in all wisdom, singing spiritual psalms and hymns and songs, with thankfulness in your hearts to God. And whatever you do, in word or deed, do everything in the name of the Lord Jesus, giving thanks to God the Father through him. (Col 3:16-17)

Everything we do, in word and action, is to be an expression of the thankfulness that flows from the word of Christ dwelling in us. As we have seen, the Bible calls

19 We are obviously passing over other key Christian emotions—in particular, peace and hope, peace being the state we now enjoy as God's friends rather than his enemies; and hope, the long view that sustains us through this life to eternity. While the focus here is to look more narrowly at the affections that give purpose to our singing, peace and hope are still great things to be singing about!

us to respond to salvation with a life of service (e.g. Rom 12:1). But here in Colossians the emphasis is different: it is on doing everything with an attitude of *thankfulness to God*.

In Christ, we have been rescued from God's wrath and redeemed to eternal life. And yes, God requires our obedience (the external response), but he also wants the internal, heartfelt response. He wants us to thank him for his grace and goodness to us; and to keep on saying it daily. If love and joy are the emotions that mirror God's own character, then thankfulness is the emotion of the one rescued from sin and death; and it is the essential emotion to flow through and out of our singing!

Singing allows us to show our gratitude in what we say, *and* teaches us to express it in what we do. Driven by the word of Christ, our songs can express the genuine attitude of the heart whilst never becoming a 'work'. It is why Hebrews can say that in Christ we should "continually offer up a sacrifice of praise to God, that is, the fruit of lips that acknowledge his name" (13:15). In Christ, we offer nothing to God but the response of our hearts. It is only when our hearts are his that our works of service will be pleasing to him. And the first work of service (seen over and over again in Scripture) is the fruit of our lips. Led by the Holy Spirit, the gospel song 'tunes our hearts to sing thy grace'.[20]

20 R Robinson, 'Come Thou Fount of Every Blessing', 1757.

So what does this mean for us?

Firstly, if your church's singing shows *no* sign of emotion (think back to the North Korean football match)—if the word of Christ inspires little joy or thanks—then I expect you'll see little thankfulness in any other part of the church's life. When we lose the gratitude the gospel inspires in us, then we will see selfishness, dissatisfaction, materialism, greed and immorality in the church, as we replace thankful obedience with self-centredness.

Expressing thankfulness, on the other hand, teaches us to avoid worldliness. That is why a renewed, grateful heart is an essential companion to godly obedience. It's why singing is vital in feeding the *right* emotions when we declare the things God has done for us in the gospel, provoking us to lives of gratitude—not worldliness. It trains us to be thankful, obedient people in all that we do.

So how should we express emotion when we sing in our gatherings? Well, there's no straightforward answer to that question! The Bible's concern is not about how much or how little we show of our emotions. It's not about whether arms should be up or down, or if there should be clapping or reverent silence. The issue is whether our affections are captivated by the gospel. Do we encourage (or even allow) our churches to be what God created them to be—a people of love and joy (and peace and hope, etc.) who respond to the gospel with genuine thankfulness? The Bible is clear that what characterizes the people of God is their praises, in their words and actions—actions that include the expression of their God-inspired emotions.

Once we get all that, we then need to acknowledge that God has 'wired' us all differently. We are all by nature emotional, but each of us will express our feelings in different ways: some with deep passion and others more reservedly. The gospel demands that we lovingly accept and nurture the personalities God has given each of us. And it *is* important that we encourage an emotional response to the gospel in the whole congregation. But at the same time I also want to think about whether my own desire for self-expression/repression needs to be tempered, or amplified, for the good of my brothers and sisters. Similarly, we need to guard against false displays of emotion driven by wanting to fit into our church culture, or by wanting to prove to others how spiritual we are.

I would suggest, however, that to display genuine and authentic gospel emotion will be costly, in the same way that it is costly to encourage others or to witness to Christ. So, while I find it effortless to express emotion when I play the piano (because the instrument is doing half the work!), to stand singing in a congregation with my heart fully engaged is actually hard work and quite threatening. Singing in front of others makes us feel exposed. And while being in a crowd and being confidently led will ease that stress somewhat, we selfishly don't want to let others know how we are being affected—even when that sort of authenticity should be a tremendous encouragement.

When we meet as a church, we should be able to be our most genuine, and by that I don't mean that we shut down our brains in order to turn on our hearts (or vice versa). Rather, singing in the church gathering is where the word and Spirit of Christ feed both my mind and my heart. It should also be an opportunity to encourage my brothers and sisters by showing them something of my own joy in salvation, and the thankfulness that the gospel inspires in me. This is the biblical model for singing.

Remember Mary's song:

> "My soul magnifies the Lord,
> and my spirit rejoices in God my Saviour,
> for he has looked on the humble estate of his
> servant." (Luke 1:46-48)

Mary praises God by recalling his deeds of mercy and blessing and faithfulness, bringing down those who stand against him. What stands out in this song is the way that the facts and feelings intersect. The truth of the gospel is what feeds the emotion of the singer: "My soul magnifies the Lord, and my spirit rejoices in God my Saviour". And we see the same thing in each of the great songs of the Bible: filled with gratitude, the singer declares and responds to the gospel with otherwise inexpressible joy.

Summary

What is important about our emotion is that is inspired by the gospel. We can't measure the status of our salvation by the way we feel, and yet if we feel nothing then we know something is probably wrong. Some churches will strive to *create* emotion because it is their only guarantee that God's blessings are real. But that emotion is driven by human experience, not godly affection, and denies God's promise to dwell within us perfectly in Christ.

The New Testament shows that accepting God's grace in Christ means feeling something about it. The gospel should captivate our affections. Christians are people of love and joy like their creator, and, because of their redemption in Christ, are people filled with thankfulness. God gives us song as a mouthpiece for the soul, for the expression of both truth and affection. But that expression will look different from church to church, as we are all wired differently as individuals and groups and cultures, according to God's sovereign design for his people.

The challenge, therefore, is not to make ourselves more or less emotional, but to encourage *authenticity* in our response to the gospel, in love and joy and thankfulness—the emotions of the saints:

> Not only that, but we rejoice in our sufferings, knowing that suffering produces endurance, and endurance produces character, and character produces hope, and hope does not put us to shame, because God's love has been poured into our hearts through the Holy Spirit who has been given to us. (Rom 5:3-5)

This leaves us with one final question to answer: Who is responsible for leading the singing? Sure, we all share in building up the church in song. And each of us is to encourage the church as we sing the gospel story with love and joy and thanksgiving. But who has the role of leading praise, guarding the truth, and shepherding the hearts of the congregation? I would suggest that this is not a skill taught in music theory lessons. It is the job of the pastor—to whom we now turn our attention.

5. LEADING SONG

People like to be led. Nations like strong prime ministers and presidents. Children like teachers who can maintain discipline. Churches thrive under the servant leadership of godly pastors. We like to be led. Strong leadership gives us confidence to play our part in a team, knowing that someone else has ultimate responsibility (and will take the blame when things go wrong!).

It is no less the case with music. An orchestra may have 100 skilled musicians on a stage, but it will only create a cacophony of sound without a conductor. In a world that can create reality TV shows out of anything, I wasn't surprised to see a program recently that took three 'celebrities' and put them in a competition to learn how to conduct and then perform with a professional orchestra. As you might expect, these unsuspecting maestros had little ability to control the music. The orchestra, trained to follow their leader at all costs, would respond precisely to the wild tempo changes and abrupt cues. And almost none of the rookie conductors could understand that to successfully lead meant anticipating the orchestra's playing. Instead they would fall into the trap of following the music, creating a 'feedback' loop that eventually slowed the whole thing to a halt. Musical leadership requires being in control and being ahead.

But leading singing in church is far more than just a musical exercise. As you would expect, the Bible shows us that leadership in the church involves very different priorities than simply getting the job done. Ultimately, the church is led by Christ. Those who hold leadership within his church do so under his authority, modelling their own leadership on his—obedient to God's commands and sacrificial in their service. As such, Jesus' leadership should influence the direction of our singing, just as with other ministries of the Word.

We have seen that it is vital to do music ministry in the way that God intends, which will see the word and Spirit of Christ building his church as our minds are filled with the knowledge of God's will, our hearts are affected to respond with thanksgiving and praise, and our bodies are equipped to live thankful lives of service. This requires, under Christ, thoughtful and deliberate leadership—not just so that our music will sound good, but so that God will use his gospel to effect love, faith and obedience in his church.

The song leader

a. Who is the song leader?

Practically speaking, when Christians are singing together, anyone standing at the front is a song leader: the pastor, the service leader, the singers. But the organ, the choir, and the instrumentalists will also function as leaders to differing degrees, depending on the style and culture of your particular church. Where there is no leadership, the congregation will look for it anywhere they can, trying to lock on to the strongest power source—and that could be the tone-deaf man in the back row singing louder than everybody else. Many of us, therefore, have a song-leading function in church. But for simplicity, let's for now just imagine one person whose job it is to lead us in song.

b. Song leaders in the Bible

In case you are thinking that song leading is purely a pragmatic role (because in many churches that's all it is), I would suggest that song leading is foremost a pastoral role. We can see this by looking at the Bible and *its* song leaders. Yes! There *are* song leaders in the Bible—but as they tend to have other (important) roles, we often don't notice the song-leading part of their jobs. The biblical song leaders are in fact not normally musicians, but the spiritual and political leaders—leaders whose job it is to lead their congregations in praise, thanksgiving and obedience.

Moses

So, for example, there is Moses. Appointed by God to be the spiritual head and governor of Israel, he is prophet, priest and (in a sense) king—essentially foreshadowing what Jesus would become. And because of his position, Moses is the one who rightfully leads his people in the song of God's victory at the Exodus:

> Then Moses and the people of Israel sang this song to the LORD, saying,
>
> "I will sing to the LORD, for he has
> triumphed gloriously;
> the horse and his rider he has thrown into
> the sea.
> The LORD is my strength and my song,
> and he has become my salvation;
> this is my God, and I will praise him,
> my father's God, and I will exalt him."
> (Exod 15:1-2)

As Israel's pastor, Moses directs the people to sing of their salvation. This song is the first action of the newly saved Israel. But it is also Moses' first job as pastor—to lead the hearts of God's people to thanks and praise.

David

Move ahead to King David. By this time, Israel's leadership structure has expanded significantly. David is God's anointed ruler, reigning on earth on God's behalf; and there are now defined roles for prophets and priests. But while David is himself an accomplished musician, the sheer scale and responsibility of governing Israel means that it is not practical or appropriate for him to be running their band practices. Rather, he appoints musical leaders. In 1 Chronicles we have the story of David leading Israel in bringing the ark of the covenant to its final home in Jerusalem:

> So the priests and the Levites consecrated themselves to bring up the ark of the Lord, the God of Israel. And the Levites carried the ark of God on their shoulders with the poles, as Moses had commanded according to the word of the Lord.
>
> David also commanded the chiefs of the Levites to appoint their brothers as the singers who should play loudly on musical instruments, on harps and lyres and cymbals, to raise sounds of joy… Chenaniah, leader of the Levites in music, should direct the music, for he understood it…
>
> So David and the elders of Israel and the commanders of thousands went to bring up the ark of the covenant of the Lord from the house of Obed-edom with rejoicing. And because God helped the Levites who were carrying the ark of the covenant of the Lord, they sacrificed seven bulls and seven rams. David was clothed with a robe of fine linen, as also were all the Levites

> who were carrying the ark, and the singers and Chenaniah the leader of the music of the singers. And David wore a linen ephod. So all Israel brought up the ark of the covenant of the LORD with shouting, to the sound of the horn, trumpets, and cymbals, and made loud music on harps and lyres. (1 Chron 15:14-16, 22, 25-28)

It's hard to comprehend what this incredible day would have looked and sounded like, when God's word is placed at the heart of the nation's life, accompanied with singing, rejoicing, processions and bands playing. As king, David leads the procession, and as such he is *the leader* of the praise of Israel. But he appoints Chenaniah for the specific task of directing the music. And it's important to note that Chenaniah is a Levite, which means he is a priest. The role was not given to just anyone—Chenaniah is both musician and theologian.

But let's dig a little deeper. Why did this moment require such celebration and ceremony? Because it was a key event in the history of salvation, where God was illustrating how his kingdom was to function. God is God, his king sits on the throne, and at the heart of God's rule is his word and law, demonstrated in the bringing of the ark to the nation's capital. And that is a matter for *great* rejoicing—which is where the singing comes in. The moving of the ark could have just been a religious duty for Israel, as God's rule *does* require the response of obedience. But crucially, it also requires the heart-response of thankfulness and joy, which is what David and his musical director are leading. To underline the importance of this role, notice that amongst the elders, military commanders, priests and musicians, only David and Chenaniah are named (vv. 25-28). Leading the nation in rejoicing was an important *and* natural accompaniment to the act of placing God's word at the nation's heart.

Now, it is totally understandable if you can't relate this episode to your Sunday service! But you and I are members of that kingdom which David and Israel could only foreshadow. The head of our church is God's eternal king, Christ Jesus, and it is by his own word that he now leads his people. And for those in Christ, our hearts exist in a constant state of spiritual celebration—because the salvation he won for us is ongoing and perfect. How much greater, then, is our salvation to that which Israel experienced in the Exodus? How much more exciting is it that God would plant his word in our hearts, rather than in a box in a temple (2 Cor 3:3)? How much richer and more radical, then, should our response be?

Jesus

Given what we have just seen, we should expect to find in the New Testament a leader of praise in the church who far surpasses Moses and David. And we do. In the eternal kingdom where Jesus rules, we find that *he* takes the responsibility to lead our rejoicing. Jesus is our Saviour King *and* the leader of our praise!

> For it was fitting that he, for whom and by whom all things exist, in bringing many sons to glory, should make the founder of their salvation perfect through suffering. For he who sanctifies and those who are sanctified all have one source. That is why he is not ashamed to call them brothers, saying,
>
> > "I will tell of your name to my brothers;
> > in the midst of the congregation I will
> > sing your praise." (Heb 2:10-12)

Ultimately it is Jesus who directs the praise of the church. He is the one who is most worthy to lead our rejoicing, having made the church perfect in his death and resurrection. He stands equally *with* us as a brother in God's congregation, and *before* us as our pastor and our king, and as the one leading our praise—our song leader.

c. Song leaders in the church

There is no greater model for leading singing in our churches, then, than Jesus himself. Reflecting Christ's example, the pastor-song leader is the one who takes the lead in preaching the gospel to the church congregation, and shepherding their hearts to respond in words and songs of praise.

But if that is case, why do so many of us (pastors, service leaders, etc.) find it such an awkward thing to lead the praise in our congregations? It is clear in the

Bible that we pastor through preaching, as we teach and apply the word of Christ, feeding faith and obedience in the church. But equally the pastor is to lead the hearts of the congregation to praise. I guess many will feel totally unequipped to take on such a role. But again this is where the Bible helps us—where we are shown that rather than abdicating all responsibility, we can delegate at least part of it, as David did with Chenaniah. The church leader needs to wisely appoint *and work with* someone who will coordinate and lead the music and praise with skill—ideally not just a musician, but someone who also knows their Bible well and has a pastoral heart. In this way the church pastor takes responsibility for what is sung and how it is led, rather than letting the music be swept along by whatever is the latest song or trend. It also means the music leader can get on and do the things they are good at: leading and encouraging the team of musicians and singers, arranging the music to reflect the truths being sung, and ensuring that in practice the congregation is being properly and engagingly led to look at Christ.

Choosing what to sing

The leading of singing begins well before any words are sung in church. It starts with the planning of services and the choosing of songs. It happens as sermons are prayed about and prepared. But ideally it also happens in a partnership. The pastor-music leader combination

not only brings both theological and musical wisdom to what is going to be sung, it also guards against the obvious problems that can arise when one person, or one position, controls the music in a church. Unlike the sermon, where the word of God is taught and applied through words alone, singing requires theological insight *and* musical skill. Getting the theology of our songs right is essential; it is a ministry of the word of Christ and therefore should be filled with same content and carry the same weight of responsibility as the preached Word:

> For I delivered to you as of first importance what I also received: that Christ died for our sins in accordance with the Scriptures, that he was buried, that he was raised on the third day in accordance with the Scriptures. (1 Cor 15:3-4)

The message of our songs is therefore of first importance. If a song doesn't deliver on the gospel, then we shouldn't be singing it. Theological wisdom in song leading is vital, and will protect the church from singing what can be popular but vacuous or, at worst, heresy.

However, a song might deliver on the gospel but be let down by the music—in which case I still wouldn't sing it! There are so many factors concerned with getting the music of our songs right: its suitability for corporate singing (or for *any* singing!); its ability to convey the emotion of the lyrics; and its contextual relevance to those you are trying to reach. Musical wisdom is vital in choosing songs that will engage hearts with Jesus; and in

protecting the church from singing the pastor's favourite choruses from when he was at Sunday school 40 years ago!

Who should be writing new songs?

Martin Luther, Isaac Watts, Charles Wesley and John Newton were not foremost musicians but pastors. But as shepherds of God's people, for them to lead singing meant writing hymns that would teach and train the hearts of their congregations. While we all do have a role in ministering the Word to one another in singing, the biblical model of song leading often sees the pastor as the lyricist—preaching God's word in poetry. It is not fair to expect that all our musicians will be trained in theology (although if they can be, that's great!). And therefore we can't expect that our musicians will necessarily be able to provide us with the rich and fresh expressions of the ancient truths that we so often long for. It is pastors who spend their time exploring Scripture, and thinking and praying through its application to life and faith. It is they who have theological gifts that can help craft lyrically excellent material for each new generation of believers.

A word of warning, however: many who set out to write new songs have it in their heads that they are writing for a global audience. Their aim is to create a hit—the same way you would with a secular pop song. That is not actually the gospel work most of us are called to. Just as a preacher's job is to speak first to the local

church, so it is for songwriters. Some pastors *will* have gifts that see them preaching to a wider audience; and so will some gifted songwriters. But if that is your aim, then you've missed the point of pastoral song leading. Writing, leading and singing gospel songs is a ministry of the local church to build itself up into Christ.

The well-led church

So what does good song leading in a church look like? Much of it will never be seen, as it will be done in the prayerful preparation of services, the wise choice of songs and, for some, the creation of songs themselves. It will happen as a pastor takes a keen and vital interest in the ministry of the Word to those in his care, as it is preached and as it is sung. But as an overseer he is also a collaborator, working with those who have both musical skill and pastoral maturity.

Those who have the task of actually leading the music will also be prepared—in prayer and in practice. The singers will model what it is to 'sing to one another'—with eye contact, and warmth, and joy, and conviction, all displayed in an authentic and appropriate manner. But their whole character will be aiming to draw attention to Christ rather than to themselves. Similarly, the musicians—playing instruments of whatever shape, size and sound—will play in order to lead with confidence, but equally to accompany. They will play remembering

that the lead instrument is the congregation itself.

And the church, feeling secure in being led well, will sing with heart. They will sing praise, and prayers, and doctrine, and doxology—each in some way recalling our salvation in Christ—with a desire to respond with thanks and obedience. They will care less about the style of music and more about serving and encouraging their brothers and sisters. They will care not about being entertained or having a 'special moment', but about being fed and satisfied by the word of Christ as the Holy Spirit plants that word in their hearts. And in some small or large way, they will be gaining a glimpse of the eternal gathering around Christ to which they have been called.

6. THE FINAL SONG

And they sang a new song, saying,

> "Worthy are you to take the scroll
> and to open its seals,
> for you were slain, and by your blood you
> ransomed people for God
> from every tribe and language and people
> and nation,
> and you have made them a kingdom and
> priests to our God,
> and they shall reign on the earth"...

And I heard every creature in heaven and on earth and under the earth and in the sea, and all that is in them, saying,

> "To him who sits on the throne and to
> the Lamb

be blessing and honour and glory and might
forever and ever!"

And the four living creatures said, "Amen!" and the elders fell down and worshipped. (Rev 5:9-10, 13-14)

Does this image reflect your normal experience of church each Sunday?

For many of us, the reality of church will be one of hard work. It will feel weak. There will be an odd assortment of people. We will struggle with each other's human frailty and tiredness and trials. And the church will have few resources to do the gospel ministry it would like to.

Some churches will aim to be like heaven on earth—but will only be artificially so. Focusing on living life to the full, such churches will appear materially successful, with outstanding music and life-affirming preaching. They will sing songs of praise not because of a first love for Jesus, and not because they are humbled by God's grace, but because they feel blessed by the feelings that accompany prosperity, beautiful people and great music. They forget that God uses the trials of this life to refine faith, to inspire rejoicing, and to create a longing for his glory (1 Pet 1:6-7).

Interestingly, a great deal of contemporary Christian music flows out of this 'successful' Christianity, and not out of the struggles of faith. Why that is interesting, and perhaps troubling, is that the Bible's songs are more often than not sung by the humble, the downcast, the afraid, the prisoner, and those who have been rescued from the brink of death. It is these saints who seem to know what it is to sing with true joy. It is these saints who are able to declare God's praise because of a real encounter with God's saving power. These saints have a genuine confidence in God's faithfulness, mercy, and power to forgive their sin. Their souls find comfort in him because living by faith demands the commitment of their hearts. God engaged with them in their deprivation, making plain his purposes to them so that:

> …we who have fled for refuge might have strong encouragement to hold fast to the hope set before us. We have this as a sure and steadfast anchor of the soul, a hope that enters into the inner place behind the curtain, where Jesus has gone as a forerunner on our behalf… (Heb 6:18-20)

The only real anchor for the soul in this life is the hope we can have in Christ Jesus, who by his own suffering and sacrifice received the right to lead the praise of the church.

So do you need to be in a mega-church to do great gospel singing? No! If anything, the more 'successful' your church, the more likely it is that your music will become a concert, quenching spiritual hunger for the moment but never satisfying the longings of the soul. Seeking the finest facilities, musicians and equipment is not necessarily going to help your church's singing achieve what God wants for us in Christ.

But while musical materialism will leave us wanting, what God provides us with is perfect. He gives us the most powerful and amazing gospel: the gospel of salvation in Jesus Christ. And what is so simple and yet so compelling about that gospel is its ability to be spoken *and sung*. You may not have a building. You may not have a piano. You may in fact be in chains for Christ. But as Isaac Watts put it:

> I'll praise my Maker while I've breath,
> and when my voice is lost in death,
> praise shall employ my nobler powers;
> my days of praise shall ne'er be past,
> while life, and thought, and being last,
> or immortality endures.[21]

Have you ever considered that the words of our songs might be the most profound words you will ever speak? They tell of the source, the sustainer and saviour of all creation. As humble as our gatherings may be, and as weak as our voices are, we are reminded in Revelation 5 that those same words are being echoed in the throne room at the heart of the universe: "For you were slain, and by your blood you ransomed people for God".

That same gospel song is being amplified by every voice of every saint and every angel in heaven. When we meet together, reminding each other to press on in the faith that we share, offering humble praise from broken hearts, and singing the word of Christ into our souls, we know that those same words are being sung before

21 I Watts and J Wesley, 'I'll Praise My Maker with My Breath', 1727 [1719].

the actual throne of God: "To the Lamb be blessing and honour and glory and might forever and ever!"

We are *all* called to this ministry—the ministry of the Word in song. It satisfies our souls, not because of what it is but because of what it contains: the living water of life in Christ. It is both beautiful and life-changing; challenging and subversive; demanding of heart and mind; and calling all to thankful service of Christ.

O for a heart to praise my God,
A heart from sin set free,
A heart that always feels Thy blood
So freely shed for me.

A heart resigned, submissive, meek,
My great Redeemer's throne,
Where only Christ is heard to speak,
Where Jesus reigns alone.

A humble, lowly, contrite, heart,
Believing, true and clean,
Which neither life nor death can part
From Christ who dwells within.

A heart in every thought renewed
And full of love divine,
Perfect and right and pure and good,
A copy, Lord, of Thine.

Thy tender heart is still the same,
And melts at human woe:

Jesus, for thee distressed I am,
I want Thy love to know.

My heart, Thou know'st, can never rest
Till Thou create my peace;
Till of mine Eden repossest,
From self, and sin, I cease.

Fruit of Thy gracious lips, on me
Bestow that peace unknown,
The hidden manna, and the tree
Of life, and the white stone.

Thy nature, gracious Lord, impart;
Come quickly from above;
Write Thy new name upon my heart,
Thy new, best name of Love.[22]

22 C Wesley, 'O For a Heart to Praise My God', 1742.

APPENDIX 1: DELIBERATE SONG LEADING

> I will tell of your name to my brothers;
> in the midst of the congregation I will praise you. (Ps 22:22)

How do we lead our churches to sing well? How do we get them to engage with Christ and each other when the music starts? How do we get our churches to the place where hearts and lives are affected for the kingdom through our singing? Like all good leadership, we do it deliberately. Deliberate song leading simply means that we lead our music with thought, prayer and intentionality. It is not just left to chance. We take time to think through how our singing fits into a service, how it complements the preached Word, and which songs will best encourage praise, prayer, teaching, encouragement and response. And we take time to think more broadly about where singing sits in the life of the church. We carefully choose the right people to stand up to lead singing, and we pray for them and help them as they prepare for that role.

This is not to say that every song we sing requires a detailed plan of execution. Some of the most powerful Christian singing happens spontaneously! However, thinking deliberately about music leading will mean that song leaders are taught how to think biblically and pastorally about the ministry they are engaged in, and then trained in whatever techniques will help them use their gifts (or lack of them!) to serve their congregation.

Showing personality

What people find easiest to engage with in you as a leader, is… you! Showing *yourself* is what helps grow any relationship, and is the first part of asking others to follow your lead. In practice it might mean projecting a bigger personality than what you might normally project. I am not suggesting we should not be authentic; authenticity is essential. But often when we follow our natural instincts in song leading, we'll take a step backwards, look down, sing timidly, and show little of ourselves. This not only hinders the congregation in engaging with you, but can also make people feel nervous and insecure—which means they will also sing timidly.

Good song leading relies on thinking purposefully about how you are communicating—having the confidence to exaggerate something of yourself in order to lead others better. This applies whether you are the main song leader, a member of a choir, or leading the singing from an instrument. Actors will say that to get into a role, they need to find something of that character in themselves and then exaggerate it to a point where they can convince an audience. Of course, in church we are not acting; in fact, it is crucial that we are not trying to be somebody else. No-one will relate to or follow someone who is a fake. So when we show emotion, it must be our own genuine response to the gospel and not something put on. But we do need to *show* it! When you model this, people will follow. They will engage with you because they will see that you believe the gospel you are singing.

Knowing the music

There is no getting around the fact that having some musical skill is an important factor in leading singing well. You are the guide as to when to sing, when not to sing, what notes to sing, what mood to sing in, and so on. So, knowing a song back to front musically is essential.

Does this mean that you need to have a degree in music before you can sing up the front? Not at all. If God can use jars of clay to proclaim that Jesus is Lord (2 Cor 4:5-7), then he can use those same jars of clay to minister his word as we sing. Factors such as congregation size, style of music and the number of available musicians may determine what level of skill is required (or achievable) for different contexts. Yes, the reality is that the more skilled you are as a musician, the better you will do at *accompanying* singing. But it might be that as the pastor of a small church, you are all there is in terms of people who can confidently stand in front of others. Or it might be that in some contexts a less musically trained person is actually better at *leading* singing. For example, the fearless and outgoing youth group leader might be the one best suited to engaging a bunch of teenagers. And ultimately, for anyone, the base level for music leadership should be dependent not on what grade you have passed but on your godliness (more on this later).

However, skilled or unskilled, you are the one everyone will be looking at and following, so practising the songs and practising how to lead is essential. And if you are part of a team, and you need more rehearsal time rehearsing to do your job better, then make sure you let the rest of the team know!

So, what if you are not really a singer or a musician but are nonetheless standing at the front of the church (because you are the service leader or similar)? Should you be at the music practices too? Ideally, yes! But if there is someone standing beside you who is the 'official' song leader, then you may need to consider stepping to the side so that the congregation knows who they should be following. (Even then, remember that everything you do up the front is modelling something to the congregation about how to sing.) Now, if you are the service leader *and* the main song leader, then yes—you really do need to practise with the musicians! Unprepared service leading looks bad enough. But unprepared song leading will undermine all the work of the musicians and lose the trust of the congregation.

Knowing the theology

It is as important to know a song theologically as it is to know a song musically. If you are the one who introduces the songs then this is even more important. Clueing us in to what and why we are singing is a crucial element in helping the congregation to engage with the gospel. (Although if you preach a mini-sermon before every song, people tend to disengage!) This means doing some preparation before the church service. Look for the themes and Bible references in the song. Even if you never get to say anything up front, it is still worth preparing in this way as it will help your focus and will help you to direct the musicians in how to play the song.

Remember: as a ministry of the word of Christ and the Holy Spirit, the leading of singing is an important theological and pastoral role, and as such it carries a higher level of responsibility than other roles in the music team. As ministers of God's word, song leaders must be servants—but equally they must be mature ministry-minded and biblically literate Christians.

Showing emotion

As we have seen in the Bible, song leaders are there to lead us in our first response to the gospel—our response of praise and gratitude to God for what he has done for us. And if you're standing at the front, then what you communicate is what you are asking the church to follow you in. If you make eye contact with people, you are encouraging them to sing to one another. If you smile, you are encouraging them to express joyfulness. Of course, there is no single 'right' way to externally show the joy and thankfulness of your heart. However, if you look down, appear disengaged, make no eye contact, or feel nothing—then the church will follow you!

Pointing people to Christ

Ultimately, all these song-leading tips are about pointing people to Christ. More important than singing the right notes is showing that your eyes are on him. Much of this will happen through the things you say. But even if you say nothing, it will always help to show something of your own engagement with the gospel as you lead. I have often thought the best church musicians are those who play not only with great skill, but in a way that draws attention away from themselves and towards Christ and the gospel.

Those musicians understand what God wants most of all: people who are genuinely and prayerfully engaged with him long before they walk up on to the platform or pick up an instrument or a hymnbook. This is the unseen part of music ministry, but it is what is most crucial for all leadership: a love of Jesus, a heart for prayer, and the attitude of a servant.

APPENDIX 2: ISSUES FOR CHURCHES

> When you come together, each one has a hymn, a lesson, a revelation, a tongue, or an interpretation. Let all things be done for building up. (1 Cor 14:26)

Concert church

Think back to what church music was like 50 years ago. In style it may have lagged behind the musical currents of the world, but what it often had right was a focus on the congregation as the main voice. Put aside any other thoughts you might have about pipe organs in church—quite simply, its job was to be the one instrument that led the many in the task of singing the gospel. Yes, organs could overstep the mark and overpower the singing, as can many modern bands. But in general, church music was largely focused on the congregation.

Two things have changed since then: the prominence of bands in leading singing, and the influence of concert-style church. And while the Christian music concert is not a new phenomenon—think of Handel's *Messiah*—with the rise of the internet and social media engagement, there is now no limit to our access to large church and conference music from around the globe. As in so many areas, developments in technology have had a profound influence on how we engage with church music. So, whether we are there in the arena, or watching on YouTube, we have now effectively become the audience—passive spectators watching the musical priests perform their rituals, as genuine and heartfelt as they might be.

Just to be clear, I don't actually have any problem with going to a concert of Christian music, or even a concert where I am asked to join in the singing. However, this is not the same as being part of the local church. For many of us, however, the line between the church gathering and concert-style Christian music has now become completely blurred.

What are the implications of this trend?

The loss of the congregational voice

Two of the key ideas about singing in the New Testament are:

1. It is always done with an eye to each other, to strengthen the church.
2. The chief (in fact only) instrument spoken about is the voice, for the obvious reason that Word

ministry involves speaking the gospel to each other.[23]

It is quite conceivable that 1 Corinthians 14 and Colossians 3 could encompass those times when we might 'perform' a gospel song—such as a solo in church, or at a concert. But as church is before anything else a 'gathering', it makes sense that "singing to one another in spiritual psalms, hymns and songs" is most normally going to be a corporate activity. Therefore whatever instruments you choose to use, they will never be as important or as necessary as the congregational voice. If church music were a concerto, then the congregation is the star solo instrument. The orchestra and conductor have a vital role in the 'performance'. But their goal is not to bring glory to themselves, but to promote and honour the 'virtuoso'.

That's not to say it is wrong to have a visual focal point in our singing. We need the helpful lead of our singers, the band or the choir. But this is an area where our thinking can easily be distorted, when we start to believe that what goes on up the front of church and the

23 Many have made the argument that because there are no instruments mentioned in connection with singing in the New Testament, we should not, therefore, use instruments in church at all. Similar is the argument that we should only sing the songs recorded in Scripture. But that's a whole other book! All I will say here is that Paul seems less concerned with the particulars of how church meetings are done, and much more with how our union with Christ works out as we act towards our brothers and sisters with love, service and humility in every area of church life.

people who do it deserve our attention and honour above Christ and his church, who we are serving. This is not helped by the video clips we see of 'concert church' songs being led by beautiful people and super talented musicians. In an age of all things visual, watching a congregation sing just doesn't make good viewing! Too easily we adopt a culture of wanting to be entertained each time we come to church. And our aim becomes to replicate the line-up of players and singers we see performing on YouTube or at the Christian conference, rather than to look first at how God has specifically gifted our own congregation. It is a common attitude that to achieve great contemporary and cool music you just need to put together the perfect band. In reality, the most helpful thing for many churches may be to take stuff out and do things simply! Plenty of great Christian singing has happened over the centuries without any instruments at all.

There is more to say to musicians about this a little later. But great singing in church is the responsibility of us all. Supporting the congregational voice needs to be at the heart of our planning, practice and performance—all of which starts with our attitudes and expectations, as we come to church with the primary goal of ministering the word of Christ to one another in love and service.

Songs that are not designed to be sung

Another problem with the 'concert church' is that it feeds us un-singable songs. Performed by the talented 'worship leader' backed with funding and exposure, the songs topping the charts will often come out of mega-churches and large conference movements. The thing about a conference, however, is that any song can work and sound amazing! The young guy with cool glasses, leading on guitar, whose voice is half an octave higher than yours, will be able to make anything go off. His pro-musician backing band will help a lot, too. And the vibe amongst the 10,000-person audience will be thrilling.

But what happens when you bring that song back home to your church? To start with, most of your congregation weren't at the conference, so they have no emotional capital invested in the song. Unfortunately your musicians can't quite pull off what the pros were doing, either. And the key the music is written in suddenly seems way too high! What is an amazing song in one setting doesn't really work in the reality of your church.

Again, this is happening because we are seeing a blurring of lines between church music and pop music. It's not that church songs can't be contemporary—but what we too easily forget, purely at the musical level, is that church music is a unique medium and always has been. If you focus on the individual at the front, then the music will lean towards suiting the individual's voice. If you focus on a choir, it's the same. When you focus on the congregation, the style of rhythm and melody will actually be very different—that is, simpler. Why is it that we can still sing hymns with far more conviction than many modern songs, as good as they are? Basically it's because a hymn has no unpredictable rhythm! There is much less thinking required for the non-musician when each note is exactly the same as the one before. There is less to remember, and therefore faster engagement with what you are singing.

I'm not at all saying that we need to avoid songs that come from conferences and large churches. But unless you are well equipped with the right musicians, song leaders and congregation, you may do a better job at serving the church by choosing material that is within your ability to do well.

The church that won't sing

Nothing is more discouraging for the church musician than trying to lead a congregation that doesn't want to sing (or at least seems not to want to sing). Here are four common reasons a congregation might appear not to be engaging with the music. I have listed them in in no particular order, although some are purely practical while others are spiritual and more serious.

A lack of critical mass

This will seem obvious, but every space requires a certain number of people to make the singing work well. This is why I have experienced far more encouraging singing in a group of ten in a home Bible study than with 50 people in a church designed for 200, or with 200 people singing outside. (The same principle lies behind why your singing in the shower sounds so good!) Just as they say that a crowd attracts a crowd, so, too, heart-driven singing improves when you feel like you are in the midst of others. Often we don't have much control over the space in which we do church—but if you do, think about the logistics of containing the people and their sound in order to make the singing resonate.

Singing the wrong songs

By 'the wrong songs', I don't mean those songs that people hate because they are 20 years out of date. What I'm talking about here has to do with the congregation's ability to sing. There is a good reason for doing the grade 4 music exam before you start learning grade 5 pieces: it can be extremely discouraging to attempt music that's well beyond your ability. And, just as an individual musician has musical ability, so a church congregation has corporate musical ability—which with practice and encouragement can actually improve and flourish. Some congregations are on the path of learning to sing better, while others are as good as they are ever going to be! But congregations in both categories often attempt to sing music they aren't up to singing. I have led some church choirs that have involved teaching each part, note by note, over a period of weeks; and others where every member can sight-sing the music with no effort at all. The latter have the joy of being able to tackle complex works and master them quickly, which is great fun. But the former still end up making great music when they sing what is within their ability to achieve.

It seems that all too often, however, we attempt music that is not within either the ability of our congregation to sing or the ability of the musicians to play. Again, are we thinking first about which songs will practically grow the church in Christ, or are we wanting to attempt songs simply because they are popular and cool in other contexts? So, while I'm not suggesting we return to a hymns-only diet, there is a rhythmic and melodic simplicity in traditional church music (and also evident in much contemporary music!) that makes it immediately accessible to any group of people. That is, it's designed to be corporate—and is therefore excellent for the ministry of word-of-Christ-in-song.

Of course, there is great satisfaction for churches that *are* able to sing complex pieces of music—but your musicians need to be competent enough to lead well in that style. Many is the time I wish I had fewer people in my church band, rather than more, because the task of leading the more challenging songs has proved too much for us—ultimately letting the congregation down.

Poor leadership

As we have said, congregations love to be led, and led strongly. No-one wants to be the one to open their mouth at the wrong time, and having confidence in those leading will alleviate that fear. When a song leader knows when and what to sing and can communicate that they are in control, the church will gladly follow. If a song leader shows fear or uncertainty, the congregation won't risk making fools of themselves. They will in fact look around for whatever the strongest power source is—perhaps the piano or guitar, or anyone who looks like they know what is meant to be happening. Just as an orchestra needs a conductor, a congregation needs a leader—and, while they needn't be the most polished singer in the world, a leader who can show confidence with joy will be a great encouragement to healthy singing.

Poor spiritual health

This is perhaps the hardest problem to cure, although it is quite easy to diagnose. Often, people in church won't sing because they are spiritually immature or perhaps spiritually dying. You might have the best musicians and song leaders in the world, but if the Spirit of Christ is not at work in the hearts of the congregation members then they won't sing. As we have seen, our singing is a ministry of the Word, driven by the Holy Spirit. If the Spirit is not implanting the truth of the word of Christ in our hearts (either because we have let them grow hard or because we just don't believe the gospel we are singing), then we should not expect that Word to provoke any heart response. Just as the crowd at a football match will sing with gusto because they believe in their team, so it is with the church. In fact, any singing (Christian or otherwise) tends to be heart-driven. The church that does not have the Spirit at work (as big or successful as it may be in other ways) will not want to express the gospel in song, and certainly will not do so with any conviction or passion.

APPENDIX 3: IDOLATRY IN CHURCH MUSIC

> But he [Moses] said, "It is not the sound of shouting for victory, or the sound of the cry of defeat, but the sound of singing that I hear".
> (Exod 32:18)

The things that give us the most pleasure are the easiest things to turn into idols and worship. And when that idol looks and feels like the real thing, it can make us oblivious to the fact that we might be serving a counterfeit god. It's an unfortunate reality that church music can so easily fit into this category.

I love leading people to sing...

Musicians already have a dangerous propensity to idolize their art, and it can get worse the more gifted you are.

There is an attitude among many musicians that pursuing musical excellence is the goal of using your musical gifts. It is a pride that leads many to look with disdain on those who are less competent than themselves.

But that pride exists equally amongst the committed in church music. I can look back at instances of leading singing where I have not had the remotest thought of serving Christ or his church, my first priority being to make sure the music is sounding brilliant. Satisfying people's expectations and receiving positive comments can easily become what I most long for when playing music in church. Sadly, this same pride has seen many talented musicians refuse to get involved in music ministry at all because of their perception that church music is too 'common', or their unwillingness to play with people less able than themselves.

Of course there are idols in every part of life (and ministry). But musicians who are good at what they do need to be alert to our predisposition to serve the creation before the Creator; and to please people rather than the Lord. As with every gift God gives to his church, we need to pray that music is used in our gatherings in service, humility and love.

Singing is like a drug

It's always hard to know what is going on inside of others when you watch them singing in church. While I worry when I see people looking completely bored, I also worry if I see them looking intoxicated with the music. Of course, it is for God alone to judge the hearts of his people. But still, there are times when I am concerned that people are loving the musical experience more than the gospel they are singing about.

I'm not wanting to suggest that musicians should play badly in order to keep an emotional lid on things. For most of us, playing badly comes more naturally than playing well! If anything, musicians need to work hard in order to encourage genuine gospel-inspired emotion in our singing. Nevertheless, it is crucial that we all keep a check on our hearts when we come to church. We need to do it prayerfully as individuals. We need to do it prayerfully as music teams and congregations. And service/song leaders need to be good at helping to focus the minds and hearts of congregations as they thoughtfully introduce and lead songs, always directing us back to Christ and the gospel.

Musicians are cool!

It is all too easy to idolize those at the front of church—whether they are preachers or musicians. There is an often-held (although completely false) perception that those at the front of church must be more godly than the rest of the congregation. With musicians there is an additional attraction of seeming to be emotionally in touch, arty, and sometimes even quite cool. Of course, if the thought of being perceived as cool leads anyone to desire leadership in the church then they are the wrong person to be leading. Christ came to serve, not to be served; and any form of Christian leadership must reflect the service of our Lord. Those serving up the front of church have to live with the constant temptation to perform for the praise of people. When you pray for the musicians in your church, pray that their hearts might be protected from pride, performance and perfection:

- Pride: possessing an attractive gift that others do not; forgetting that Christ is the one who gives gifts to his church, when and how he chooses, in order that the body might be built up in him.
- Performance: exercising your gift in order to win the praise and acclamation of others. Admittedly, this is how most of us are trained as musicians—to perform. But in the church, this whole idea is turned upside down as we are to use our skills in order to point people to Christ rather than ourselves.
- Perfection: serving the music itself—a temptation that gets stronger the further you climb the musical ladder.

APPENDIX 4: CHURCH MUSICIANS

> I will sing praise with my spirit, but I will sing with my mind also. (1 Cor 14:15)

Who should serve in music ministry?

Someone who loves Jesus as Saviour and Lord! While this may seem like common sense, it is not at all uncommon for non-believers to be filling bands and choirs, playing organs, and singing at the front of churches. This might be because they feel they are doing their 'community service', just as they might help with the church's flower arranging. Or it might be that the anxious pastor is looking for a way to keep fringe people actively involved in the congregation, whether or not they are genuinely saved. Or, worse still, it might be that the pastor cares more about how the music sounds than about the hearts of the musicians and the example that is being set.

My argument against this practice is the argument of this book. The music leader is a minister of the word of Christ. We don't invite just any gifted speaker (newsreader, politician, stand-up comedian) to preach the sermon to our congregations; neither should we invite non-believers to serve in this vital ministry.

Not that every role has the same responsibility, of course. The clarinettist is not going to have the same pastoral role as the song leader; yet they will still understand something of the purpose of Christian singing, and let that influence the way they play. They will come to church knowing that their role is to serve the body rather than perform to the body.

What if you don't have the musicians/singers/ leaders you want?

As we have noted, the Bible gives us no indication of what the ideal church music group will look like. But we can see for both theological and practical reasons that congregational singing, as it mirrors God's bigger picture for the church, will ideally have a leader. In fact, plenty of Christian singing down the centuries has simply used a song leader with no instruments. And, while I think a song leader is always going to be the first and most crucial position in a music team, the support of a harmonic/rhythmic instrument (e.g. piano, organ, guitar) is always going to give a congregation extra confidence to sing.

But do you really need more than these two (or one, if it is the same person)? Well, there is no single answer that makes sense for every church. But a small team of confident music leaders will always be preferable to a large team of dubious ability. In my experience, the more musicians you use, the more chance things will go wrong. And, as with any musical ensemble, the overall sound of the group will only be as good as its weakest member. I'm not at all saying not to go for a large band if you have excellent players and/or an experienced leader. But don't ever think you can't lead great singing with only one or two confident music leaders. You'd be surprised how well a stripped-back ensemble will work for any sized congregation!

What if you don't feel you are good enough to play in church?

Despite what you think, the congregation isn't actually listening out for all the mistakes you are going to make. They just want to be led. And there is one word that has transformed music across the centuries: practise! Practise your instrument, practise singing, practise how to stand in front of others. Practise in order to serve Jesus and his church.

ACKNOWLEDGEMENTS

Much thanks goes to those who have helped get this book from ideas to print: to Alyson Grove for arranging a lot of random ideas into a coherent narrative; to Tony Payne, Samantha Dunn and Emma Thornett for insightful comments, suggestions and improvements to the manuscript; to Andrew Lubbock for his constant support in this ministry; to the Emu team—past and present—for giving me a job that allows me to think about all this stuff; to the musicians of St Ebbe's, with whom it is a privilege to serve, and who will know more than anyone how far below the ideals of this book I fall!; and most of all to my family for just being them.

Feedback on this resource

We really appreciate getting feedback about our resources—not just suggestions for how to improve them, but also positive feedback and ways they can be used. We especially love to hear that the resources may have helped someone in their Christian growth.

You can send feedback to us via the 'Feedback' menu in our online store, or write to us at info@matthiasmedia.com.au.

Matthias Media is an evangelical publishing ministry that seeks to persuade all Christians of the truth of God's purposes in Jesus Christ as revealed in the Bible, and equip them with high-quality resources, so that by the work of the Holy Spirit they will:

- abandon their lives to the honour and service of Christ in daily holiness and decision-making
- pray constantly in Christ's name for the fruitfulness and growth of his gospel
- speak the Bible's life-changing word whenever and however they can—in the home, in the world and in the fellowship of his people.

Our resources range from Bible studies and books through to training courses, audio sermons and children's Sunday School material. To find out more, and to access samples and free downloads, visit our website:

www.matthiasmedia.com

How to buy our resources

1. Direct from us over the internet:
– in the US: www.matthiasmedia.com
– in Australia: www.matthiasmedia.com.au

2. Direct from us by phone: please visit our website for current phone contact information.

Register at our website for our **free** regular email update to receive information about the latest new resources, **exclusive special offers**, and free articles to help you grow in your Christian life and ministry.

3. Through a range of outlets in various parts of the world. Visit **www.matthiasmedia.com/contact** for details about recommended retailers in your part of the world, including www.thegoodbook.co.uk in the United Kingdom.

4. Trade enquiries can be addressed to:
– in the US and Canada: sales@matthiasmedia.com
– in Australia and the rest of the world: sales@matthiasmedia.com.au

5. Visit **GoThereFor.com** for subscription-based access to a great-value range of digital resources.

Also from Matthias Media

Sing for Joy

6 topical Bible studies by Nathan Lovell

Music and singing are wonderful gifts from God that seem strangely destined to cause frustration and grumbling in Christian churches around the globe. Why does something so good create such problems, and what does God have to say to us about our singing?

Sing for Joy is a set of six studies that look at what the Bible has to say about why we sing and how we sing as God's forgiven people.

This book will help you to delve into the Scriptures to think about the nature of praise and worship and how to encourage each other as you sing together.

The final two studies are particularly targeted towards those in music ministry, to help them think through the implications of what the Bible has to say about music for their role in serving the body.

An ideal study book for individuals and small groups.

Available for purchase from Matthias Media or for download from **GoThereFor.com**.